REIMAGINE INCLUSION

REIMAGINE INCLUSION

DEBUNKING 13 MYTHS TO TRANSFORM YOUR WORKPLACE

MITA MALLICK

WILEY

Published by John Wiley & Sons, Inc., Hoboken, New Jersey.
Published simultaneously in Canada.

For general information on our other products and services or for technical support, please contact our Customer Care Department within the United States at (800) 762-2974, outside the United States at (317) 572-3993 or fax (317) 572-4002.

Wiley also publishes its books in a variety of electronic formats. Some content that appears in print may not be available in electronic formats. For more information about Wiley products, visit our web site at www.wiley.com.

Library of Congress Cataloging-in-Publication Data is Available:

ISBN 9781394177097 (Cloth)
ISBN 97813944177110 (ePub)
ISBN 97813944177189 (ePDF)

Cover Design: Wiley
Author Photo: © JWJ Photography

SKY10053137_081023

For my parents:

Satya Priya Mallick & Manjula Mallick

"I love you big like the sky."

Contents

Introduction

My entire life I have been chasing inclusion. Because I have never really felt that I belong.

I am the proud daughter of Indian immigrant parents, who left everyone and everything they knew behind in Kolkata, West Bengal. My younger brother and I were born and raised in the United States, in a time and place where it was not cool to be Indian. I was the funny looking dark-skinned girl with a long, funny looking braid, whose parents spoke funny English. We listened to funny sounding music and ate funny smelling food. Until it wasn't funny anymore.

Growing up, I was bullied by my peers, both verbally and physically. They let me know every single day that I didn't belong. While I didn't feel included in our small and mostly white community, I also didn't see myself included in the greater world around me. Not on the small screen or big screens, not in books and magazines, and not on the shelves of our local grocery store.

I quickly began to understand that I was different. And yet I desperately wanted just to be included, to be part of the community like everyone else. So I thought studying hard and studying some more, achieving straight As and extra credit, winning awards, and receiving accolades would be the key to being included. I knew my capabilities, and I knew I was capable of more. And I believed my relentless drive to learn and make an impact would be the key to my success in Corporate America.

I quickly found myself struggling as I started my career as a marketer. I was eager to learn the technical aspects of the job and picked those up quickly. Although I enjoyed the actual work, I was completely overwhelmed by what Michelle Obama once described as the "everyday paper cuts" so many of us who look "different" experience on a daily basis. Every single exclusionary act, small and big ones in the workplace building on top of one another, left me questioning if this was the organization I was meant to work for. Because just as I had during my childhood, I didn't feel included. I didn't feel valued, seen, or recognized. I left one organization for another, in search of better bosses, better titles, and better development opportunities. All along, I was chasing inclusion.

After close to two decades of working across sectors and industries, for large and small public and private companies, it took me too long to realize this: I had been trying to thrive in workplaces that were never built for people who look like me. And these structures, processes, and systems didn't just magically appear. They were predominately built by people who didn't look like me. Leaders who for most of their lives had known what it felt like to be included in their workplaces. In some cases, they didn't regularly experience, see, or understand what exclusion was.

So, I transitioned from a successful career in marketing—where I had fought to ensure people who looked like me were included and represented in products, services, and content—to working in the field of diversity, equity, and inclusion. Once again, chasing inclusion. This time not just for myself, but what it means for leaders on their journey to be more inclusive. What it means for organizations on their journey to build more inclusive cultures. And finally, the ripple effect organizations can have on the greater ecosystem—the positive impact they can make when they actively practice inclusion, and the consequences they have to face when they don't understand the harm and hurt exclusion can cause.

Over the last several years, I have seen the growing interest in diversity, equity, and inclusion efforts. I have watched leaders and organizations spending billions of dollars on diversity, equity, inclusion, justice, and belonging, all while arguing over the meaning and order of those words. Many have hired Chief Diversity Officers, only to then cut this work, reinvest in it, and then cut it again. They are blaming the lack of diverse pipelines for not being able to increase the diversity of representation of their workforce and pressuring Employee Resource Groups to do more. Confused as to why there aren't more people of color in the C-Suite. Some of these same leaders, who are white men, struggle privately or publicly with Diversity, Equity, and Inclusion (DEI) efforts, feeling that their voice simply doesn't matter anymore. And finally leaders scrambling on what major event, devastation, crisis to address, when and why, asking this question: Is this about politics or is this about human rights?

As I have been chasing inclusion over many years, I have developed deep expertise in this space. I have coached hundreds upon hundreds of leaders. I have led organizations through many a DEI crisis. I have been the confidante to many a CEO, founder, and board member. I have participated in countless keynote speeches, fireside chats, and panels. I have worked with both large and small companies. I have shared my thought leadership in social media platforms, on my own podcast and other podcasts, and in major publications and news outlets. And yet, I am not a self-proclaimed DEI expert. Because I don't believe, in a world that changes so quickly, that we can be experts anymore. I just have deep DEI expertise.

As I continue to build my expertise, I approach this work embracing humility, a constant drive to gain more empathy and understanding for experiences that aren't my own, and a commitment to meet leaders where they are in their inclusion journey, in hopes of moving them further along in their journey during their time working with me. My hope is that this book helps more leaders and as a result more organizations make meaningful progress in actually transforming their workplaces.

As you read this book, I also know there are a number of good books that have been published and are currently being published on the topic of DEI. Given my expertise, I wanted to tackle the one thing I haven't seen others address head on: the myths that we hold on to in our workplaces that prevent us from making meaningful progress in DEI efforts. We have all grown up with myths, stories that are based on tradition. Some myths we can point to being tied to factual origins. Some myths are completely fabricated, simply made up. They can explain to us why we are here, give us a sense of purpose, reassure us, guide us, and even become part of our traditions and embedded into our families and our greater community.

In this book, I'll share with you the 13 myths, which, over the many years doing this work, I have watched leaders cling to, believe, and share with others as if they were factual. These myths can spread quickly within an organization, taking over how we individually think, operate, and the decisions we make having consequences at scale. These 13 myths, if not debunked, will have a devastating impact on our workplaces. Reimagining what inclusion looks like in our organizations starts with understanding why these myths are just that—myths.

In debunking the first three chapters, Myths 1, 2, and 3, we tackle some of the foundational skills we need to continue to develop on our journey to be more inclusive leaders. We talk about the work we need to start doing outside of workplaces and starting at our kitchen tables, with practical ways to practice inclusion on our teams, and the role we need to play in having courageous conversations on race. In Myths 4, 5, and 6, we tackle some of the ways in which we can influence and help build systems and processes in our organizations that are fair and equitable. We discuss how our own biases undermine the efforts to build and uphold inclusive infrastructures. We also discuss the importance of language in DEI work and remembering our responsibility to educate ourselves on language that is constantly evolving.

In Myths 7 and 8, we tackle the unintended consequences of believing that we are doing everything we can to support our employees, including examples like launching mentorship programs and offering maternity leave. In Myth 9, we tackle how white men feel excluded and how we must include them in DEI efforts. In Myth 10 and Myth 11, we tackle pride washing and diversity washing in products and content and discuss in-depth racist ads in the marketplace. In Myth 12, we tackle the importance of both personal and public apologies and what we can do to continue to rebuild trust after we apologize. And finally, in Myth 13, we tackle what we need to do to ensure the future of the work is indeed inclusive for us all.

You will find that each myth starts with a story. Many of these stories may sound familiar to some of you, something you may have experienced or witnessed at work. We examine the myth and spend time debunking it. Then we discuss practical ways in which you can start to transform your workplaces. I leave reminder tips at the end of each myth to help you think about how, starting tomorrow, you can show up at work differently.

As you read this book, I encourage you to take notes, come back to sections that made you uncomfortable, and review concepts you didn't understand when you first read them or you disagree with. Invite colleagues to read this book with you. Discuss these myths and do the work together to hold yourselves accountable. Treat this as a leadership handbook, as your personal resource guide you can come back to when you are in doubt of something you are facing in your workplace.

If you are a white leader reading this book, some of what I say might surprise you, make you pause, question what you are reading, or make you feel unsettled and uncomfortable. I hope you can work through the discomfort to unlearn some of the things you believe to be true about DEI. Your organizations are counting on you to think about how you can show up differently at work and make an impact. And if you are someone from a historically marginalized community reading this book, much of what I say might not surprise or unsettle you, or make you feel uncomfortable. For most of your career, you have likely experienced the things I share. The burden is not on you to educate your colleagues. And if you are looking for new ways to reach them, I hope this book offers a different way to do that.

Finally, I'm often asked why I continue to do this work. Why even write this book? I continue to do this work for one simple reason—for my children, Jay and Priya. For my nieces, Emma, Lily, and Julia, and my nephew, Zachary. I do this work for all of our children in hopes they never doubt that they belong. So they won't have to reimagine what inclusion looks like because they will know what it's like to be included from the very beginning: to be valued, seen, and recognized. And in return, they will include others in whatever they choose to do in life because we all deserve to be included in our workplaces, in our communities, and in our greater world.

REIMAGINE INCLUSION

1

Of Course I Support Black Lives Matter. Why Are You Asking If I Have Any Black Friends?

"I need your help posting this image on LinkedIn," a senior white leader I had worked with said to me, repeatedly tapping at an image on his iPhone. "And how do I do the hashtag? Black Lives Matter. . .?"

I stared at the image. And looked at him. I stared at the image again.

"This image says *Stop Killing Us. Black Lives Matter.* Is this the image you would like to post?"

"Yes, I want people to know I support those efforts."

I paused and let the silence creep in for several seconds. "Have you considered using a different image? And what would you like to say? Because this image says *Stop Killing Us*, and I don't think—"

"I don't know," he interrupted me. He sighed, growing increasingly more frustrated with our conversation.

"Have you thought about what your Black friends and colleagues would like to hear from you? Have you talked to them about how you can be supporting them?"

"Oh, this is ridiculous!" he shouted at me. "I just want to get this posted before my next meeting. And of course I support Black Lives Matter. Why are you asking me if have any Black friends?"

He stormed out of the room. I sat there, staring at a crooked frame on the wall, which proudly displayed the company's values. *"Integrity. Positive Impact. Commitment. . . ."* Hmm. Well, I technically never asked him if he had any Black friends. Did I?

In the days, weeks, and months following The Diversity Tipping Point™[1] (as coined by Diverse & Engaged as the period beginning May 29, 2020, when Corporate America acknowledged Black lives DO matter), I was inundated with requests from mostly white leaders on what they should say and what they should do in the wake of George Floyd being murdered. And, of course, could I help them quickly post something on their LinkedIn or Twitter accounts so they could let people know they cared?

In my time coaching over hundreds of leaders on diversity, equity, and inclusion (DEI) topics, I have come to realize this one singular truth. Inclusion doesn't start at our conference room tables; it starts at our kitchen tables. It starts in our homes, in our extended families, and in our communities. I have spent time with white leaders, many of whom genuinely wanted to be an ally for the Black community and to loudly say that "Black Lives Matter." Some of these leaders pause in conversation with me, think for a bit, think some more, and then quietly confess, "Well, no, I guess I don't have any close friends who are Black." Because many of us continue to live self-segregated lives. We are afraid to say this part aloud. And this is the myth we have to debunk: It's hard to say you genuinely support the Black community if you actually don't have a meaningful relationship with someone who identifies as Black.

Who Are Your Friends?

In September 2019, I remember my social feed being inundated with the biggest piece of news *ever.* The *Friends* twenty-fifth anniversary. I was overwhelmed by the headlines: *Friends* hits big screen for twenty-fifth anniversary! The Top Ten Ross Gellar Moments! 25 Things You Didn't Know About Friends! Friends: 13 New Behind-the Scenes Stories! A Pottery Barn Friends Collection is coming!

The show debuted on NBC on a Sunday evening in 1994, and quickly took American culture by storm. Critics raved how relatable the characters' lives were—how the cast become so close. How these lovable characters even became friends with their viewers.

Rachel. Chandler. Phoebe. Monica. Ross. Joey. Six friendly white faces staring back at me with big, wide smiles. I had never watched the show; they were not my friends. As I stared at their photos, all I could think was: is that what everyone else's friends looked like? Where were all the friends who looked like me? Where were the Brown and Black faces? Where were all the people of color?

Friends. Sex in the City. Girls. And Greta Gerwig's *Lady Bird.* Our screens are filled with stories of white communities, white friendships and relationships, and white joys and struggles. Much has been written about the lack of diversity behind and in front of the camera, whitewashing of stories and experiences. And it starts with the storytellers.

"I really wrote the show from a gut-level place, and each character was a piece of me or based on someone close to me. And only later did I realize that it was four white girls," said Lena Dunham,[2] creator of the popular HBO series *Girls.*

Dunham's comments were honest, candid, and revealing. There was no whitewashing of experiences or stories here. On screen, she brought to life her predominantly white existence, a life likely surrounded by the comforts of white friendships and white relationships.

Unlike Dunham, Greta Gerwig has remained largely silent on the criticism she received for her award-winning film *Lady Bird* on being glaringly white. Gerwig's attempts to include people of color in the film, two specifically, falls into the stereotype of how people of color have historically been portrayed on the big screen; silent and watchful, there to highlight and support the journey of the main white character. Ironically, the film is set during 2002 in Sacramento, the same year in which Sacramento was named America's Most Diverse City,[3] and yet this diversity was noticeably not reflected in the film.

In interview after interview, Gerwig has said the movie is loosely based on her life, but far less autobiographical than viewers realize. Gerwig never had anyone call her by a different name and never dyed her hair bright red. She did, however, grow up in Sacramento. Elizabeth Bergman of *Time* magazine wrote about *Lady Bird*: "In Lady Bird, on movie screens from Sacramento to Brooklyn, women and girls are seeing themselves reflected in all of their warts and glory." It is clear that it is white women and white girls who saw themselves reflected in Gerwig's whiteness and her largely white experiences.

Guess Who the Baby Is?

As I was reflecting about *Friends*, and the sharing of stories of white experiences, I was reminded of a significant moment in my career. We were preparing for the long-awaited launch of baby products. To celebrate the launch, colleagues decided to create a game for their division called "Guess Who the Baby Is?"

On a very large wall, individuals were encouraged to bring in their baby pictures and post them on the wall. Picture after picture, cute, cuddly, and crying babies lined the wall. On the surface, it seemed like a wonderful way to create internal momentum and excitement for a big moment for the company.

"I am uncomfortable putting my picture up there," confessed one of our Black colleagues to me one morning. "There's only a handful of us on this floor. What should we call this game? Guess who the Black Baby is?"

They were right. A sea of cute, cuddly, and crying white babies lined the walls. My picture, or anyone else's Black or Brown baby picture, would have disrupted the sea of whiteness, and it wouldn't have been too difficult to win the game: Guess who that Black or Brown Baby is?

And yet this simple game, created by white colleagues, reflected their own childhood experiences and upbringing. They didn't see anything wrong with the game or understand why anyone would not want to participate. For them, it was as simple as identifying babies who all looked like them growing up, smiling white faces framed with golden locks secured tight by a bonnet. That baby game serves as a reminder of how a simple game based on our own upbringing and experiences of being surrounded by those who look like us can lead to our colleagues feeling excluded.

As I go back to the experiences in coaching white leaders on their urgent need to publicly show up for #BlackLivesMatter, it leaves me with this question as we all scramble to create inclusive work cultures: How can we expect to show up and be inclusive leaders in our workplaces if we live the majority of our lives in communities surrounded by people who only look like us? In the United States alone, we spent about $8 billion dollars[4] on diversity training. Educating leaders on issues of diversity, equity, and inclusion has certainly come a long way since the late 1960s and 1970s, when training started being held in corporations as a reaction to and to protect against expensive civil rights lawsuits. Title VII of the Civil Rights Act of 1964[5] was a landmark civil rights and labor law in the United States, which made it illegal for organizations to discriminate in hiring,

termination, promotion, or compensation based on race, color, religion, sex, or national origin.

According to Dr. Rohini Anand and Mary-Frances Winter, in their paper on the history of corporate diversity training, "most training during this era was primarily a recitation on the law and company policies, a litany of do's and don'ts and maybe a couple of case studies."[6] For most organizations, the trainings were a one-time event, ranging from an hour to four hours. There was no discussion on how changing behaviors, on how being a more inclusive leader, could lead to better business results.

In 1987, *Workforce 2000*,[7] a book published by the Hudson Institute, was one of the main catalysts for the diversity industry being born. *Workforce 2000* accurately forecasted the changes organizations would see in their workforces as the demographics of the United States shifted. It was the beginning of understanding what workforce diversity would mean and how organizations would, in their journey, either tolerate, celebrate, or simply reject the diverse backgrounds and life experiences people would carry with them into their workplaces.

Almost a decade later, in 1995,[8] implicit bias, or unconscious bias, was defined by psychologists Mahzarin Banaji and Anthony Greenwald. Banaji and Greenwald also created the IAT (implicit association test), which allowed everyone to assess their biases, and at the time it was revolutionary. The duo introduced the now well-known term *implicit bias*, which referred to "any unconsciously held set of associations about a social group." The marketplace for diversity training then over time morphed into Unconscious Bias Training for all.

When I coach leaders, I remind them that unconscious biases are learned stereotypes that are deeply ingrained, automatic, and influence our behavior. We learn these stereotypes from a young age from our families, our communities, and in our schools, like famous storytellers Lena Dunham and Greta Gerwig did. We learn these stereotypes from watching Disney Movies, from both CNN and Fox News, and from TikTok and YouTube influencers. We learn these stereotypes and internalize them based on one single interaction we had a very long time ago with someone who doesn't look like us or who isn't from "our community."

We store those memories away in our brain, compartmentalize, and categorize groups of people. When we are multitasking, when we are stressed, and when we are short on time, our unconscious bias kicks in and we make decisions influenced by our bias. We pull upon a single memory, a single story, a single conversation that has formed our stereotypes. And then make a decision influenced by our deep-seated biases, many of which are hurtful and painful to read or say aloud:

Black women can be angry and overly aggressive. Black men may not have as strong a work ethic and can be lazy. Hispanic/Latina women can dress inappropriately at work and speak Spanish better than English. Latino men can have explosive tempers and have illegal immigrants in their families. Asian men can't be very strategic and do not succeed in non-technical fields. Asian women can be modest, deferential, and don't have strong social skills.

White men play golf, can be less qualified, and steal credit from all to get ahead. White women can be self-absorbed, shallow, and will shove women of color aside to get a rung ahead on the corporate ladder. Mothers can be less committed to their jobs. Gay men can be flamboyant and effeminate. Lesbian women can have masculine leadership styles and have their own bias against men. Veterans can be unstable and unreliable, suffering from post-traumatic stress. An individual using a wheelchair can't be in a sales role because they aren't able to travel as easily. And how can anyone who is visually or hearing impaired work in a technical role?

And remember that stereotypes we harbor aren't always negative. In fact, stereotypes can be positive. And yet these positive stereotypes continue to tell false stories and perpetuate a false narrative about a community and group of people and be just as damaging as negative stereotypes.

Mothers are superheroes. Gay men are more creative and are impeccable dressers. Women are kind and empathetic. Asians are great at math and engineering. Black men are great athletes. And Black women—well they are simply #BlackGirlMagic. (P.S. Black Girls aren't magic, they are simply human.)[9]

We All Have Biases

It's undeniable and indisputable that each of us have unconscious biases. We walk into our workplaces every day carrying them with us. We rush to the next meeting while quickly sending that email to our boss and responding to those two other texts, while scrambling to meet the noon deadline—we all make decisions as quickly as possible, influenced by our unchecked unconscious bias. Imagine the devastating consequences that can happen within an organization when our collective unconscious bias goes unchecked. This can have system-wide ramifications.

We hire people who graduated from the same college we went to because we fundamentally believe our school builds the very best leaders. We coach people informally as we catch a Sunday football game together and connect over our love of the NFL. We promote those who remind us of ourselves, because we know for certain they will be as successful as we are.

Well, the solution becomes a four-hour training on Unconscious Bias Training. We ask some questions; we make some effort to participate. A basic training may cover some of the following: What does unconscious bias mean? Are there different types of biases? When does bias show up at work? How do I know if I have unconscious bias? Wait, are you sure we all have bias?

If we are fully engaged and not on our phones, we have some aha moments. We might think about it as we log off, or on the commute home, and wonder what's for dinner. We then go back to our homes, and our communities, surrounded for the most part by people who look like us.

We have no real opportunity to break through our biases, practice and apply what we have learned (because we don't have enough meaningful cross-cultural relationships allowing us to erase stereotypes), or get to know individuals, one-on-one, on a human level. We continue to rely on one article we skimmed on our phone, one show we binge-watched on Netflix, and one interaction we had in a virtual happy hour.

The only real way to shatter stereotypes in our head is to expand our social circles. A long-standing theory in the field of social sciences referred to as "contact hypothesis" says just this: connecting and building relationships with those of other races can help you gain a better understanding of someone else's experiences and to help you act on their behalf. So it's no surprise then that studies show[10] that white individuals building relationships with Black individuals directly correlates to white individuals supporting, and then actively becoming involved in, the Black Lives Matter movement.

So when I coach individuals, here are some of the questions I ask them regarding their social circles. I specifically ask them to observe who else is around them in these scenarios:

Where do you live, and who are your neighbors? Do you socialize with them?

Who cuts your hair? Where do you buy your groceries? Where do you go out to eat?

How do you spend your weekends? Who do you spend them with? What activities do you do?

(continued)

(*continued*)

Who attended the last community celebration you can remember? A birthday party, a wedding, or a funeral celebrating a loved one's life? Can you picture who was there?

Who is in your trusted circle? Who are your closest five friends you rely on?

If they all look like you, act like you, and think like you, you are self-segregating.

According to the Public Religion Research Institute's 2013 American Values Survey—the most recent comprehensive study of race and social circles—data shows that a full 75 percent of white Americans have "entirely white social networks without any minority presence."[11] The same holds true for slightly less than two-thirds of Black Americans.

"This country has a pretty long history of restriction on inter-racial contact and for whites and Blacks, even though it's in the past, there are still echoes of this," said Ann Morning, an associate professor in the department of sociology at New York University, of a 2013 Reuters/Ipsos poll that showed 40 percent of Americans and 25 percent of non-white Americans have no friends of another race. "Hispanics and Asian Americans have traditionally had less strict lines about integrating."[12] It is clear that we all need to travel beyond our current networks and social circles and break out of our self-segregation.

How to Start Building Cross-Cultural Relationships

As you start to build cross-cultural friendships, here are some key "watch-outs."

Stop Being Color Blind　"I'm color blind,"[13] a colleague had confidently proclaimed to me several years ago while we were meeting. "I'm color blind, and I don't see you as any color at all," she boldly claimed again, sitting right across from me and staring me straight in the eyes. All the while slowly sipping her cup of coffee. I stared blankly at her "First Coffee, Then Slay" gold mug.

"I just don't see color."

Color blind is the infamous get out of jail card, a free pass, a VIP status, to buy, pass go, and collect your $200 Monopoly-style and to let everyone know there's no possible way that you see color. The first "watch-out" is let's stop being color blind. If you proclaim to be color blind, you can't have any meaningful cross-cultural relationships.

When you use the words "I am color blind," you completely shut down any possibility of having a conversation with me around race. Because I am Brown. As a Brown person, I don't have the privilege of saying I am color blind. I know when I walk into my workspaces and workplaces, my Brownness has entered the room before I have even had the chance to sit down and say hello. I wear my Brownness every single day of my life.

And for many people of color, race has defined us since the day we were born. Because for us, being color blind is a privilege we cannot afford.

To invest in cross-cultural relationships, you have to see and embrace who people are. You have to see color. Because to not see color is to deny the person their identity and their very existence. So please stop being color blind. Please start to see color. Please start to see them and hear them.

Stop Thinking Having "One Friend" from Another Community Is Enough

The second "watch-out"—having one friend who identifies with another race, culture, or community—just isn't enough.

"My dentist, who I love, is Indian."

"My neighbor is Mexican, from Mexico. He has a green card of course."

"My best friend from fifth grade is Black."

"My grandchildren are half Asian."

"Did I mention my college sweetheart was Colombian? So I can't possibly be a racist. And I am one of the most evolved, open-minded people you will ever meet. I live in Manhattan, after all."

I had a white colleague who would always talk to me about her dentist Raj, who was Indian. Dr. Raj celebrated some festival with lights. Dr. Raj once had round, white Indian sweets in his office, ironic for a dentist. Dr. Raj spoke another language, started with the letter G, she couldn't remember, hopefully it would come to her. Did I happen to speak another language with a letter G, she would ask me inquisitively. I would shake my head no.

"Do you know Dr. Raj?," she asked me on more than one occasion. Because all Indians apparently within a 25-mile radius should know each other. I thought about asking her if she knew my dentist Dr. Richard, who also happened to be white, but I didn't have the energy to start that conversation.

My white colleague never did the work to get to know me as an individual and try to build a meaningful cross-cultural relationship. She came into our conversations with stereotypes she had about Indians based on one relationship she had with Dr. Raj. If she had taken the time to get to know me, she would have discovered I have never celebrated Diwali, and I do celebrate Christmas. My all-time favorite dessert is the McDonald's soft-serve ice cream cone. And I speak Bengali, not Gujarati, fluently. And for me, it became too exhausting to combat her "harmless, well-intentioned stories about being Indian"; I would simply shut down on most days and on some days manage to politely smile in response.

So remember that this one friend, colleague, relative, dentist, connection, does not prove you don't have any bias or are not racist. It does not give you a superpower or the authority to be an expert on this other community just because you have this one relationship.

If what you have absorbed in passing conversations or observations is superficial, you will only reinforce dangerous stereotypes for yourself and others. Just like you don't represent, speak to, or know all the views of your community, your best friend who is Black doesn't represent the entire Black community. The key is to broaden your social circles and make multiple, deep, cross-cultural relationships.

Finally, Start Building and Investing in Relationships

The third "watch-out" is not to let the idea of tokenism stop you from reaching out and starting to build meaningful relationships with people who don't look like you, don't act like you, and don't come from your community. Tokenism is the idea that you are making only a symbolic effort and that your efforts to connect with someone of a different race are not genuine or true. How can you ensure developing a friendship with someone of another race is not viewed as tokenism?

Start with reminding yourself of your intentions to ensure this is not tokenism. Ask yourself why you want to build new cross-cultural relationships now. Why are you doing it? Are you doing this for yourself so that you can convince yourself you have "made an effort"? To make yourself feel better, over whatever guilt you are experiencing, realizing the privilege you hold? Or is it because you truly want to broaden your social circles, and that you want to gain insight and understanding into experiences that are not your own?

As you build your new friendship, think of the strongest friendships you have had in your life and why those friendships have lasted so long. The first step in building any relationship is to be authentic and be yourself so you can get to know each another. Listen to your new friend, and let them know they are being heard, that you understand their point of view. Communicate honestly, openly, and consistently. Celebrate and find the things you have in common and at the same time, try new things together. If you are authentic, empathetic, and consistent in maintaining and developing your new friendships, you avoid collecting "token" friends and will build genuine friendships that will enhance and bring joy to your friend's life and to your own.

Finally, you will make mistakes as you build cross-cultural relationships. And that's okay. When you have made a mistake and hurt your new friend, admit it. Learn to apologize authentically. (We'll tackle the importance of apologies more in depth later in the book.) Remember, friends forgive friends.

Start challenging who is in your trusted circle and why. Friendships help define us. They can influence so many of our choices: from where we live to what we buy, and ultimately, informing us of our values and opinions on what we believe.

So who are your friends? If they look like you, think like you, and act like you, it's never too late to start investing in more meaningful relationships. This is the first step to be a more inclusive leader. It's time to find some more friends—and venture outside of that Friends' Central Perk Coffee Shop.

The relationships you invest in and take the time to grow in and outside of work is critical on your journey to be a more inclusive leader. You must audit and assess what your own life experience has been like up to this point, and whether your experiences have been largely similar to those you have surrounded yourself with. With concerted effort over time, you must have access to life experiences that are different from your own so you don't hold on to that one story, that one movie, that one experience that defines how you see an entire community. All of this ultimately helps inform whether or not you show up as an inclusive leader, and how you really define inclusion. So if you say you care about Black Lives Matter, and yet you don't have any Black friends, that matters. It matters a lot more than you think.

Starting Tips for Building Meaningful Cross-Cultural Relationships

- Actively put yourself in situations where you won't meet people who look like you. Instead of volunteering at your local synagogue, church, or temple, consider volunteering at one in a different neighborhood, town, or city, for a different organization, with different demographics. Get out of your comfort zone.
- Look for and attend different cultural events in your area. If you are anxious about attending alone, bring a friend with you. In our virtual world, there's access to so many great events online. Attending virtual events is a good way to begin meeting new people if you are having trouble building these connections in person.
- Support and shop at businesses owned by founders of color. If visiting in person, get to know the owners and chat with customers you might be in line with. Just don't stop by one time; make it part of your routine. If online, leave a positive review. When giving gifts, buy from founders of color; this is a good way to help those in your life expand their social circles as well.
- If your children have meaningful cross-cultural relationships, use this as a springboard to spend time with their friends' families, and in their communities.
- Be more active on platforms like LinkedIn, Instagram, and TikTok to diversify your networks. Like and comment on others' posts to start to nurture a connection. Message someone you don't know who you would like to get to know better. Send them a sincere note on something they shared that you appreciated. Ask them if they would like to have a virtual chat.

(continued)

At work, join and attend events sponsored by your DEI team and Employee Resource Groups. Employee Resource Groups (ERGs) as defined by Gartner are "a voluntary, employee-led diversity and inclusion initiative that is formally supported by an organization. ERGs generally are organized on the basis of common identities, interests, or backgrounds with the goal of supporting employees by providing opportunities to network and create a more inclusive workplace."[14] Get to know colleagues you have never spoken to before. Don't let that one conversation be the only time you talk. Make a concerted effort to keep in touch over virtual coffees and lunches to further nurture the relationships.

- Finally, if your trusted circle of friends looks like you and acts like you, let them know you are looking to intentionally build cross-cultural friendships. Challenge them to think about who is in their own trusted circles and why. Inspire them to join you in investing in meaningful relationships with individuals who identify with a community other than your own.

MYTH 2

I Always Allow Everyone to Speak in Meetings. Of Course I Am an Inclusive Leader.

"Yes, Greg is absolutely right about his observations. Well done, Greg," a former boss often said, showering our colleague Greg with praise when he chimed in with his thoughts.

One of my former bosses had this inclusive practice: Whenever a topic was being debated, a proposal being presented, he would invite everyone to speak. But with this invitation, there was no passing or abstaining; everyone was required to say something. He would first go around and start with those who were virtual. We all knew this was going to happen at every team meeting; we each scrambled on what we would say and how to say it. Best-case scenario and what frequently would happen: He would compliment and applaud Greg, even if what Greg said didn't make much sense. Greg was also one of the only men on our team. And our boss would then usually ignore and not acknowledge what anyone else said. Worst-case, he wouldn't just publicly disagree with what one of us said but make comments that undermined and mocked our contributions. "Mita, seems like you need a refresher on the principals of organizational development. But that's okay, we know you are not a real Human Resources professional anyway."

That year, when management asked our team to pilot and attend an overpriced, company-endorsed workshop on how to be an inclusive leader, my former boss smirked in response. "I always allow everyone to speak in meetings. Of course I am an inclusive leader. I could write the book on how to be inclusive."

From Korn Ferry[1] and Catalyst[2] to Harvard Business Review[3] and Deloitte,[4] there have been countless studies on the key traits of inclusive leaders. So many leaders, including that former boss, believe the myth that they are inclusive simply because they believe they let everyone speak in meetings. But what really makes a leader an inclusive leader?

It's the elusive question we all seem to be trying to answer as organizations continue to scramble to figure out how to create inclusive workplaces. It is because inclusive leadership is the foundation upon which great company cultures are built. When people feel they are included and belong, they are able to be the best version of themselves at work and are able to contribute all of their ideas freely and openly. They are able to make a significant impact for the company and for themselves. And even on the days they don't feel their best, they still feel welcomed and accepted by their teams. So one of the important ways we can focus on being a more inclusive leader is to start by reminding ourselves of something we have all experienced at one time in our lives: What it feels like to be excluded.

Do You Know What It Feels Like to Be Excluded?

My former boss's way of "practicing inclusion" was a flashback to memories of my elementary school gym class: kickball. Each game started the same way. The gym teacher would choose two captains. Each captain was allowed to build their own team, going back and forth to choose players, as the students lined up against the wall waiting to be selected, until all the students had been picked and the game could begin. The gym teacher likely thought this was an inclusive approach. Let the kids feel like they have oversight over the game. Allow them to build camaraderie as they assemble the teams. Continue to learn to work with others and do our best, because it doesn't matter if we win or lose.

For years, I would stand on the sidelines saying a quiet prayer I wouldn't be picked last. I stopped praying to be appointed a team captain. If I was second to last, that was a good day, because it meant I was liked better than the other alternative for the captains. For most of the games, I was last. "Ah not, Mita," the team captain who was stuck with me would groan loudly. "She can't kick the ball far at all!" One day, the gym teacher tried to help by letting me sit the game out. I read on the sidelines while everyone else played. This only confirmed the fact that I sucked at kickball and shouldn't be playing. To this day, I detest kickball.

Remembering a Time You Weren't Included . . .

- Do you remember a time you weren't included or didn't feel like you belonged?
- What specifically happened that made you feel excluded?
- Did anyone else notice how you were feeling?
- If you could go back to that moment, would you have expressed to someone how you were feeling?
- What would be the pros and cons of speaking up to say you felt excluded?

Our workplaces can reflect much of what happens in a seemingly innocent elementary school game of kickball. At work, we can be excluded because of our perceived lack of abilities. We may be labeled as being difficult or loud or taking up too much space. We may not be included because we are too quiet and never contribute. And we can also be excluded because we are just different than everyone else in almost every superficial aspect. We look different, we dress differently, we just act and think differently. All of those reasons and more are ways in which we unconsciously or consciously don't include people when it comes to the small and big moments that matter: That email. That meeting. That presentation. That leadership offsite.

One of the popular inclusive leadership models in the marketplace belongs to Deloitte, one of the world's largest professional services network. Deloitte's model[5] highlights six signature traits of inclusive leaders, which include commitment, courage, cognizance of bias, curiosity, cultural intelligence, and collaboration. The model summarizes the detail of these traits and their importance in being an inclusive leader. And here's what so many of these models miss: rather than only focusing on key traits, we need to focus on clear actions individuals can take to be more inclusive leaders in the workplace. We need to move from the academic and theoretical discussions of inclusive leadership to the practical applications, where our teams see our inclusive behaviors in action.

In my time coaching leaders, and personally experiencing many moments of exclusion, I started to think about the practical ways we can show up to ensure our teams feel included. I landed on a simple framework around three pillars I try to practice and share with others who are on a journey to be more inclusive leaders: Access, Amplify, and Advocate.

Start by Providing Access

Providing access starts by giving individuals a seat at the table. Whether this is an invite to a meeting, being appointed to work on a specific project, or the opportunity to meet with a company executive, we as leaders need to provide access. Access is the starting point for our teams to understand we hired them for a specific reason. That we value their expertise and their skills. Ultimately we want them to have access in our workplaces so they feel included.

Access can start with that infamous meeting invite. When it comes to meetings, most leaders would agree we need fewer of them, and when we do hold meetings, they need to be much more efficient. One argument I have heard repeatedly throughout my career: invite fewer people to meetings to make them more efficient. But what we fail to acknowledge is that the ways in which we conduct meetings are fundamentally broken.

Team meetings and stand-ups. Brainstorming sessions. Off-sites. Regardless of what label you give it, including people in the art of the corporate gathering is a key part of inclusion. In today's world of hybrid working, where some of us are in the office and some are remote, there's no reason to not extend an invite and include someone at the virtual table. In many cases, we no longer have to cram into a small conference room, drag in chairs, or offer someone a seat on the radiator.

Start by checking tomorrow's calendar, and ask yourself who is invited to certain meetings and who is not? Have they helped prepare materials for what's being discussed? Are they a key stakeholder for the topic being discussed? Do they have a stake in the outcome of the meeting? So why aren't they included?

To be clear, I am not arguing that everyone is to be invited to every type of meeting or gathering. I am arguing that leaders need to use meeting invites as a tool to drive inclusion. Here are three ways to think of invitations to meetings:

The Host: You invite someone on your team to host a meeting. This is an opportunity to recognize the work they have been doing, and for them to share learnings, progress, or to get buy-in to help drive decision-making. With your support, they lead the meeting.

The Contributor: You can invite someone to a meeting because they are a key contributor on the project. Simply put, if they are doing the work that's being discussed, they should be included. They should be in the meeting.

The Observer: You can invite someone to a meeting to observe and learn. You can let them know that's their role in the meeting, and let other attendees know as well. If you ask the observer to take notes, ensure this office work doesn't fall on the same person over and over again. Encourage them to jot down "key takeaways and next steps" versus "meeting minutes." You can elevate the observer who is seemly just "taking notes" by having this individual send out their observations to the group post-meeting. In this way, they can receive credit and recognition, and is one way to also start amplifying the voices of others.

Finally, giving someone a seat at the table without understanding the impact can backfire. A few years into my marketing career, I was invited to a meeting for a brand I didn't work on. I wasn't given any details, except to attend. I walked into a large room of about 15 marketers and agency colleagues. I scanned the room and immediately felt a pit in my stomach. It was clear why I had been invited and given access to the meeting: I was the only person of color in the room where they were discussing a beauty product targeted to women of color.

This is called diversity propping: using one individual from a community you are looking to serve as your proof point that you have covered all bases and have the right voices at the table. When teams engage in diversity propping, they are falling into the trap that one individual, one influencer, one spokesperson represents the voice of an entire community. The intent may be to ensure they have representation at the table. Yet, those who sent out the invitation fail to recognize the impact on the individual: the burden and the weight of having to be the anti-racist or anti-sexist check or to ensure you are being inclusive. Finally, this individual can feel tokenized, that they were only asked to be involved because they check a box, and not for their talents and expertise. It has the exact opposite effect of feeling like you are included and you belong.

In my example, the leader running that meeting could have avoided diversity propping by letting me know ahead of time why I was being given access to this meeting. He could have explained his intent: they valued my talent and expertise, and the views I brought with my life experience, and wanted me to have a seat at the table. The leader could have let me know they were focusing on diversity of representation, so I wasn't surprised and didn't feel tokenized when I walked in the room. And if I had declined to join, the leader should have respected my decision to not attend the meeting. If the leader had explained his intent ahead of time, I would not have felt negatively impacted: feeling hurt, confused, and tokenized.

Understanding Intent vs. Impact

Intent is when you want to convey or express something to someone else. This could be expressed through words or actions. Even when we don't intend to express ourselves, our silence can also be interpreted as inaction, a lack of interest or care. It can be misunderstood as negative intent.

Impact is the effect or influence you wish to have. This could be on a particular person or a group of individuals. There are people who may purposely set out to have negative impact,

(continued)

(continued)

and to hurt and harm others. I believe that in our workplaces, many of us have positive intent and wish to have positive impact. But often we get caught up in our positive intentions, and we don't stop to think about how the other person will feel and how they will actually be impacted.

So even when we set out to have positive intentions, we must remind ourselves that intention isn't the only thing that matters. We need to spend the extra time to ensure our intent matches the impact felt by others. Here are three questions to ask ourselves when considering our intentions vs. impact:

- What is my intent here? What do I hope to achieve?
- Have I considered what impact the other person will feel? Will the intent match the impact? If I'm not sure, can I stop and ask others for advice and guidance?
- What can I do to ensure my positive intent lands with a positive impact?

Amplify Voices

Too many times in my career I have been given a seat at the table, but my voice didn't matter.

Earlier in my career, I remember being invited to our annual brand plan presentation. I went to sit in the front of the room and was immediately scolded by my then manager. "Take a seat at the back, please," my brand manager told me. "We want to ensure all the leaders have a seat at the table," he said, pointing to the very back of the room, a corner where there were a few folding tables and chairs.

I had arrived early that morning to set up the room for this annual presentation. I ensured the technology worked; that we had enough printed copies; that there were enough samples for our new launch to test and try. In fact, I had worked tirelessly on the presentation when my manager decided to take the week off leading up to the presentation to go on spring break with his family. And while I was invited to the meeting to do all of the set-up, I wasn't actually given a seat at the table.

I sat in the back at the folding table and in a folding chair, silently fuming. I felt like a child who had been instructed at Thanksgiving dinner to sit at the kids' table in the corner. In the end, there was plenty of room at the "adults-only" table as I watched from the very back. That afternoon the president of the division walked by me in the hallway. He had attended the brand plan presentation earlier that morning. He stopped as he saw me approaching him.

"Nice work," he said, smiling. "Next time, you should sit at the table," he suggested.

"Yes, thank you," I smiled back, clenching my teeth at his friendly suggestion. Maybe he should have told my boss that.

Giving someone a seat at the table is only one part of showing up as an inclusive leader. In the case of that former boss, he invited me to the meeting, but didn't give me a seat at the table. He didn't want me to speak up or contribute, despite the fact that I had built the annual brand presentation. He signaled that by asking me to sit all the way in the back corner, where I couldn't be seen.

Amplifying the voices of others is a key part of being an inclusive leader. Here are three practical ways to think about how you can amplify the voices of others on your teams:

Allow the Space for All Voices to Be Heard

In the case of a meeting, invite everyone to speak and contribute. Please don't give someone a seat at the table and then not allow them to contribute. Don't relegate them to the back of the room or ask them to stay off camera. If you are planning to do that, then don't invite them to the meeting.

As in the case of my former boss, some leaders will abuse their power and force their teams to contribute on the spot. Don't put individuals on the spot and make them contribute if they aren't comfortable or aren't ready. Consider sending materials out ahead of time, where people can have the space and time to prepare their thoughts. Give them the option to contribute their thoughts in writing. In the case of projects or initiatives, working on shared documents offline is another way for individuals to comment, share, and ask questions in writing without feeling the pressure to have to contribute on the spot or in the moment.

Finally, the hardest part of leadership is listening to views, questions, or proposals you don't agree with. We must create the space for opposing viewpoints and perspectives to be heard. The journey to becoming an inclusive leader requires having an open mind and being able to actively listen to viewpoints you might not agree with. Even if you are the final and sole decision-maker, allow yourself to listen, to really hear the things you didn't expect to be discussed. Allow yourself the opportunity to change your mind.

Give Individuals Credit for Their Work

Give credit where credit is due. If individuals have done the work, they deserve to present and share their ideas in the meeting. If they did all of the hard work, why shouldn't they get to present and get credit for their work? Why are other leaders presenting their work instead? Not giving individuals credit and recognition for their contributions is the quickest way to devalue them, demoralize them, and to exclude them. They will wonder: Why do I even work here? Do I really belong here?

In some cases, leaders purposely take away the credit and recognition. These types of leaders tend to be insecure, lack confidence, and also lack competency. They may not want their team members to receive praise and recognition; they want the credit and spotlight for themselves even when they haven't done the work. You can combat against these types of leaders by doing the following: advocate to include people in meetings to present their own work. (Remember, they don't always have to stay for the whole meeting; allow them to come in and present what they are working on.) If you see someone else taking credit for work they didn't do, intervene. Ensure the appropriate individuals are credited. If this can't be done live or in person, you can always do it in writing, ensuring the person gets the accolades they deserve.

Finally, taking or stealing credit for someone else's work isn't just about taking someone's proposal and presenting it as your own. Taking credit for someone else's ideas happens all day in our workplaces. In fact, I have lost count of the number of times I have been the target of "hepeating" in everyday interactions.

What is "hepeating"? It's when a woman shares an idea in a meeting that is ignored, dismissed, or falls flat. Then later in that meeting, a man repeats that same idea and it's applauded, praised, and celebrated. The term went viral a few years back when astronomer and physics professor Nicole Gugliucci tweeted about "hepeating,"[6] a term she credits one of her girlfriends for coming up with.

When we see hepeating in action, it's our job to intervene and ensure the right person is credited. Here's some language you can use to intervene:

"Adam, thanks for elevating Mita's suggestion, which she brought up at the beginning of the meeting. Mita, let's circle back to you so we can hear the suggestion again from you."

"Adam, I appreciate you reminding us of Mita's idea. She mentioned that earlier when Chris was giving us a status update. Mita, can you tell us more about how you think we could implement this?"

"Adam, great, glad you liked Mita's recommendation so much. Thanks for repeating it and reminding us all. Mita, anything you would like to add?"

The goal is to publicly acknowledge the person whose original idea it was, and circle back to the person, giving them the opportunity to speak again to reclaim their idea.

Actively Facilitate

As leaders, we must actively facilitate, guide discussions, coach through tough conversations, and sometimes, be the referee. Just like in the hepeating example, we need to step in when we see others being excluded. Don't allow individuals to talk over or interrupt each other. Don't allow one person to take up all the airtime and take over the meeting. Do interject and do interrupt when you need to take back control of the meeting. Here are some helpful prompts to consider using:

"Mita, I understand you are passionate about this topic, and you have spoken a few times. Let's give space for others to speak. Let's pause and invite someone else to contribute."

"Mita, we appreciate your insights, and we are focused on a different topic today. Who else would like to give their views on the decision we need to make?"

"Mita, thanks for your contributions. In the spirit of making space for others, I would ask you to send me a follow-up note with any of your ideas or schedule one-on-one time with me to discuss further."

Remember, you don't have to be the most senior person to do any of this. We all need to stand up for each other to create an inclusive environment where we all feel like we are recognized, seen, and valued.

Be an Advocate

Ultimately, we all need to advocate for each other in our workplaces. And particularly, as leaders, we must recognize we have more power than some of our team members do. So it becomes even more critical that we champion, support, and sometimes fight to make sure individuals aren't being repeatedly left out or left behind. Here are some practical ways in which we can advocate:

Ask How You Can Help

Don't make assumptions. If you see someone being excluded, check-in with them. In the case of my elementary school gym teacher, he took me out of the kickball game thinking he was being helpful. In the end, sitting on the sidelines only made me feel worse. Brainstorm ways you can help and ask them how they would like you to get involved.

Ensure Equitable Distribution of Office Work

Office work has expanded as many of us work in person and work remotely. It can include everything from ordering lunch, setting up the room for a senior leadership meeting, passing around samples, sending invites, tracking attendees, and dealing with technical difficulties. Scheduling virtual happy hours, in person gatherings, or being "volun-told" (when you are volunteered to do something without your permission) to organize a baby shower, bridal shower, or going-away party. Ensure this burden of office work is shared, and pitch in to help yourself. Don't expect the same people on your team to do the office work. Because what we might not realize is that each time that same person orders lunch, takes notes, and deals with the technical difficulties, it takes time away from them being included on meaningful and impactful work that can help develop their careers.

"Say My Name When I Am Not in the Room"

Ensure you are crediting and recognizing people even when they are not in the room. Say their names. Get other leaders to understand their value and worth. Share their track record of success to ensure they are included: in that meeting with CEO, appointed to that task force, or considered for that next promotion. As my career sponsor Gail Tifford once told me, some of the biggest decisions leaders may make about your career happen behind closed doors, when you are not even in the room. (We will tackle the importance of sponsorship more in depth later in the book.)

For those leaders who have a seat at the table when career decisions are being made, be an advocate. Say their names. And remember, any one of us can advocate for someone else in an organization. You can send their boss an email praising their work. You can credit them in a meeting they aren't in. You can publicly thank them at a gathering. When we advocate and fight for each other, we build a stronger sense of community built on mutual admiration, respect, and trust. And that's something we all want to be part of.

Remember that becoming a more inclusive leader is a continuous journey. There's no destination we are rushing to arrive at; there's no competition to win to see who can be more inclusive; there's no scientific way, no precise indicator to measure how inclusive you actually are. Each and every small act of inclusion makes our teams feel valued, seen, and recognized. When it comes to making sure your talent doesn't walk out the door, forget those free fancy snacks, those meditation apps, and that fitness reimbursement perk. Because being an inclusive leader is one of the biggest ways we can retain and develop our talent.

Starting Tips on How to Run an Inclusive Meeting

- Who is on the invite list? Are they clear about their role as an attendee?
- Who haven't you included? Why? If someone else is leading the meeting, can you review the invite list with them?
- Are you able to send out materials ahead of time?

- Are you able to ask for contributions and feedback in a written format?
- Are you introducing individuals during the meeting so others are clear as to why they are there?
- Are you allowing individuals to share their own work?
- Are you making space (literally) for individuals to sit at the table? Are you welcoming them and inviting them to sit next to you?
- Are you or someone facilitating the meeting? Assign someone to facilitate to ensure all contributions are valued.
- Are you prepared to intervene and interrupt when necessary to ensure everyone can contribute if they would like to? And to ensure ideas are credited appropriately?

Inclusive Meeting Reminders in a Hybrid World of Work

(We will tackle how to build inclusive environments in our hybrid world of work more in depth later in the book.)

Many of us find ourselves in meetings where some of us are in person, and some of us are online. Here are some reminders of how to host inclusive meetings in a hybrid world of work:

Do you have best practices for hybrid meetings? For example, are all participants in the room also required to log into Zoom or Microsoft teams so participants online can see them as well? Do you ask all participants to ensure they have their names listed on the screen?

Do you have time to do quick introductions, so you can understand who is in person and who is online?

(continued)

(*continued*)

Are you monitoring the chat function for comments and questions, and responding as needed? Are you ensuring all participants have an opportunity to speak if they want to, both in person and those online?

For large gatherings, are you asking attendees to say their name before asking a question or making a comment? Introducing ourselves and saying our names to each other creates community and a sense of belonging.

Starting Tips on How to Have Inclusive Interactions

- Before a meeting starts, listen and watch out for the banter of what people are discussing. Are you talking about the NFL Draft? How are the kids doing with back to school? Are you discussing joining a local soccer league? Watch for these casual topics being discussed and help expand the topics to include more individuals. Focus on topics like weekend or vacation plans, what shows people are watching, or restaurant or recipe recommendations.
- Remember to pick inclusive team-bonding experiences. (You may recall the "Guess Who The Baby Is" game that we discussed earlier which left colleagues of color feeling uncomfortable and in some cases, feeling forced to participate.) Some may not be comfortable with basketball, soccer, or volleyball. While a manicure, pedicure, and blow-out spa day may be welcomed by some, others may feel excluded. Activities surrounding alcohol for those who don't drink can feel isolating, and engaging in excessive alcohol use can

be a recipe for disaster. Consider bonding around card games, sharing a meal together, puzzles, and board games. Survey team members for ideas as well on what they would feel comfortable engaging in.

- Finally, be aware of how much time you spend with individuals. If you casually meet one team member for golf every Friday, how does that make others on the team feel? Even if you invited them and they don't play golf, think of other ways to connect with them one-on-one to help them feel included. Time is the most precious commodity we have as leaders. Make sure you share your time equally and fairly so everyone knows they have a place in your organization.

It's Time to Have Some Courageous Conversations on Race. Let's Ask Our Employees of Color to Lead Them.

"Let's get the Black Employee Resource Group to share how they are feeling with our senior leadership team," a former leader said. "Let's get them to share their personal stories. Let's ask them to lead the conversations. Go ahead and get it scheduled."

I sat there in silence. I was hesitant, and, honestly, unable to articulate why we shouldn't do this.

"Don't you think this will make our Black colleagues uncomfortable?" I blurted out, as this leader got up from his desk and started to make his way to the door. "If we ask them to do this . . ."

"Why would this be uncomfortable? For who?" He said, raising his voice.

"I just think there may be another way, what if we . . ."

"Just watch, senior leadership is going to love this," he had snapped at me. "This will be moving and powerful. I know what I am doing, I have a good instinct for these things. Call it Courageous Conversations on Race."

It was the summer of 2016. Alton Sterling has been shot and killed by police officers on July 5, 2016. Philando Castile had been shot and killed by police officers on July 6, 2016. Our Black colleagues, rightfully so, had wondered why most of leadership had stayed silent when it came to the killing of these two Black men. The leader, who was white, had a very common reaction to our Black colleagues wanting an all-white leadership team to acknowledge the killings of Sterling and Castile: put Black colleagues' pain on display for the benefit and education of the white leaders. Because anytime a historically marginalized community is hurt or harmed, it's their job to educate mostly the white leaders in the organization. The burden is on them, and usually the Employee Resource Group, to do this work. Not the white leaders.

The leader ended up "inviting" 15 Black colleagues to share their feelings about the killings, their own stories when it came to police brutality and the criminal justice system. We sat in a very large circle, including the members of the Black Employee Resource Group, the white senior leadership team, and me. This leader gave a speech at the beginning, mostly for the white leaders, for them to feel safe in this space. For most of the 60-minute circle, I felt nauseous as I listened to Black colleagues share their pain, never losing composure, while many of the white leaders sniffled, gasped, or had tears streaming down their faces. I went from studying people's shoes, looking at the clock on the wall, to glancing around the circle and finally back to the shoes again. I still remember staring at a leader's navy shoes. This leader passed Kleenex around to his peers. I guess he had come prepared.

Afterwards, we munched on potato chips and sandwiches as if nothing had happened. Some leaders couldn't stay for lunch and awkwardly left. Afterward, I never spoke to any of my Black colleagues about how they felt about that day. I was embarrassed and ashamed. I wondered if they felt they even had a choice to decline the invitation, knowing that each of them were junior in the organization. When Stephon Clark was killed by police officers on March 18, 2018, seven months after this powerful conversation, I don't recall any of the white leaders who were in the room addressing Clark's killing with their teams. It was like that original, powerful storytelling circle had never happened. To this day, being part of that gathering is a moment I still regret. I wish I had more political capital, power, and courage at the time to stop that conversation from happening the way it did.

Who Is Actually Being Courageous, During a Courageous Conversation on Race?

Courageous conversations seem to be one of the latest trends sweeping the world of diversity, equity, and inclusion, particularly when it comes to racial inequity. The story I shared is much more common than we realize, happening on smaller and bigger scales across organizations. For some of you, while the characters and setting are different, the plot of the story rings eerily true. And for others who read through this example, you may be struggling to understand what's wrong with it. It sounds inclusive to me, doesn't it? Why not have people of color in our organizations lead conversations on race?

Let me offer the following four things for us to reflect on:

First, white leaders asked Black colleagues from the Black Employee Resource Group to come and share how they were feeling about watching Black individuals being killed. I used the word "asked" as opposed to "invited" because this is how power dynamics can work in organizations. When senior individuals ask junior individuals to do something, there's not much room to say no, without potentially dealing with repercussions. Too often, we put the burden on Employee Resource Groups to drive our inclusion agenda. Because when the latest horrific headline fills our social media feed, of loss of life and harm caused to an individual and a community, we then have our Employee Resource Groups on speed dial. We ask and expect those from historically marginalized communities to rise above the pain and trauma they experience and teach us about their pain and trauma. It is not the job of your Employee Resource Groups to run your diversity, equity, and inclusion (DEI) agenda. And to make sure everyone else, who doesn't understand the harm inflicted, feels comfortable and included discussing these difficult topics. Your Employee Resource Groups cannot be your DEI strategy.

Second, the comfort of the white leaders was more important than the Black colleagues. The objective was clear: to ensure the white leaders were as comfortable as possible, and to make this whole experience easy for them. To shield and protect them from having to do too much during the session, if anything. They didn't speak. They sat there shedding tears and listening to the pain that was on display. We brought the stories to them, because it would have been too hard to Google the pain the Black community was feeling, particularly during the summer of 2016. Hearing the stories all together, as the leader kept noting, would make it all the more powerful. But as we discussed earlier, if these white leaders had meaningful relationships with Black individuals, there would have been no need for this circle moment.

Third, we didn't expect anything from our white leaders after this session. Some of them didn't even stay for the lunch, which was our futile attempt to foster some new relationships. We were trying to shield and protect them for having to do too much, either during or after the session. Months later, one of our Black colleagues shared with me that one of the white leaders would see them in the hallway and not even acknowledge them. They would awkwardly rush by or pretend to be on their phone. "Even after THAT conversation we had, not even a smile or a wave."

Finally, the whole notion that this was a courageous conversation on race was simply not true. Because, according to the Merriam-Webster dictionary, courage is defined as having the "mental or moral strength to venture, persevere, and withstand danger, fear, or difficulty."[1] Conversation is defined as an "oral exchange of sentiments, observations, opinions, or ideas."[2] In this case, only our Black colleagues practiced the two c's, making it really just a one-way dialogue. The irony is that for most people of color, we have been having "courageous conversations on race" all of our lives. While others may deem them courageous, we don't always have a choice to not be courageous, to not engage. These conversations are weaved into our everyday existence, experiencing some of them at a young age.

When's the Last Time You Had a Courageous Conversation on Race?

My very first courageous conversation on race I can remember was with Anna. I was six years old. I remember that my younger brother, parents, and I lived in a neighborhood where our home was at the end of a cul-de-sac. There were about 40 houses in this neighborhood. We were one of the only families of color who lived there. As a first grader, I didn't really understand what that meant until that summer afternoon conversation with Anna.

Anna, a fellow first grader who was white, lived three houses down. That summer, she had gotten a new pink bike with a flower basket. She was zipping around that neighborhood with a group of white kids and me, gathering at her driveway. "Who wants a turn?" Anna shouted gleefully, whizzing past and then turning around, braking right in front of the crowd. The kids shrieked, waiting patiently in line for a turn. I also joined the line; I was excited to try her bike. I waited patiently watching one kid after another going around the cul-de-sac and coming back.

Just as I was about to get on the bike, Anna stopped me.

"You can't ride my bike."

"I was waiting in line for my turn," I replied, confused.

"My parents say I am allergic to the color of your skin. So you can't ride my bike."

"Huh?" I replied, confused. "What do you mean?"

"Just what I said. My parents say I am allergic to the color of your skin. So you can't get on my new bike."

"Is that . . ."

Anna didn't let me finish. "Come on, Molly, you're next," she said.

I stood there frozen. I felt like a bee had just stung me. And I was recovering from the shock of the sting.

"Oh, ok," I said quietly, feeling uncomfortable and anxious. "I am sorry," I added quickly, as I moved away for Molly, the blond girl with pigtails behind me, so she could get her turn. I watched that little girl whizz away. I stood there for a while with the kids, lingering and unsure what to do. After several minutes, I walked home. I felt sad continuing to stand there watching everyone else take turns.

That was the very first "courageous conversation" on race that I can recall having as a child. It quickly taught me this: I was different from everyone else. I didn't have the language to express what that meant. In fact, at the age of six, I ultimately believed Anna when she said her parents told her they were allergic to the color of my skin.

At the same time, it made me sad and anxious. When I tried to question her and engage in discussion, she wasn't interested. She knew what her parents told her to be true. And I felt I had done something wrong. I had somehow harmed her. And I don't recall ever sharing that story with my parents because I felt ashamed.

At a young age, I was slowly socialized to believe the following: to offer a lukewarm opinion, suggestion, or rebuttal, but ultimately accept what white peers were telling me to be true. To not make them feel uncomfortable. Their comfort was more important than mine. And if somehow I did make them uncomfortable, or more specifically that my Brownness made them uncomfortable, to say "I am sorry." "Sorry my lunch is smelly" or "Sorry you can't understand what my parents are saying." Apologize and move on.

For most people of color in the United States, we encounter racism from a young age. And as my friend Dee C. Marshall says, we call things by their right name. That childhood encounter wasn't a microaggression; it was racism in action. But in our communities, and in our workplaces, we avoid words like racism, white supremacy, and white privilege. Because microaggression is a more digestible term: a microaggression may be a comment, a question, a joke that's made unconsciously and not really said on purpose; it can be subtle or not so subtle, never really intended to cause harm. The person who said the microaggression didn't know what they were really doing and just needs some training. Now the term racism—that's a heavier pill to swallow. The belief that certain races are superior to others? That we treat people unfairly because of the color of their skin? This is still happening today? Nah, let's go back to microaggression. It feels just a bit more warm and fuzzy.

And unfortunately, too many leaders make this mistake: thinking inclusion is synonymous with comfort. That it should be easy; it shouldn't be difficult or uncomfortable. Because if you have been included for most of your life in almost every work situation, it's hard to acknowledge or understand that you haven't experienced much discomfort. You don't recognize that pit in your stomach, that knot in your throat, or that dull headache that comes on from realizing you don't actually belong in this space. So in that case, having a "courageous conversation on race" may seem like a daunting, insurmountable task where you don't want to say or do the wrong thing. Because if you have entered the world of work, and this is the first time you are confronted with having a conversation on race, then start by acknowledging this: you hold privilege. You had the privilege of never having to address, discuss, or think about race.

What is Privilege?

When working with leaders, here's how I like to describe the word privilege. It's a benefit, right, advantage, or favor you have. You may have been born with it. You may not have asked for it; it's out of your control that you have it. You may go most of your life not even realizing you have it. Until someone points it out, or you are forced to acknowledge it. You can have privilege or not have it because of your gender, sexual orientation, wealth, ability, religion, and, of course, race, among many others.

But the idea of privilege around race, particular white privilege, can be triggering to some white leaders. One white leader once shouted at me, "I have had a tough life, no one ever handed anything to me! My mom was a single mom and we were on welfare. Don't talk to me about privilege!"

I explained to this leader in a subsequent conversation, when he was ready to hear it, the following: Having white privilege, or any type of privilege, doesn't mean your life has been easy. You may have lacked privilege in many other ways and no one is denying that. What I am asking you to consider is if your race, if

---

being white, has ever held you back in your career. Because if you can understand that you hold this privilege, it's the first step in thinking about how you can show up as a more inclusive leader at work.

Ultimately, it can also be difficult to acknowledge the privilege we may hold, because we don't want to be painted as racist, someone who is solely responsible and being blamed for the current system. Because we haven't intentionally done anything to hold anyone back. Remember that the term white privilege is not designed to make anyone feel guilty, bad, or question their accomplishments and contributions. To learn more about the concept of white privilege, please read Peggy McIntosh's widely read article: "White Privilege: Unpacking the Invisible Knapsack."[3]

When it comes to discussing race at work, let's remember the following. No one is asking you to write a dissertation on race relations. No one is asking you to go on television and share your opinion. No one is asking you to figure out how to put an end to racism. Here is what more and more employees are asking you to do: As a leader in the twenty-first century, be culturally aware. Understand what's happening in our world. If harm is caused to our community, check-in on us. See how you can support and help. Because the silence can be deafening.

How Can You Reach Out to Colleagues Who Have Experienced Trauma or Pain?

We have established that putting colleagues of color on display, asking for them to share their trauma and pain in front of a majority white audience in our workplaces, should not be something we ask for or pressure anyone into doing. (If anyone wants to share their story on their own, support them in creating space to do so.) Instead, focus on the ways you can check-in on colleagues, showing up with empathy, kindness, and respect. This can apply to any colleague who has personally experienced pain or trauma, or whose community has been the target of harm and hate. It's too easy to blame the company or the CEO for not sending out a mass email or sending a message too late. It's far more difficult to take ownership of personally acknowledging and checking in with colleagues.

When I coach leaders, I approach them with these three options: The one-on-one Check-in Message, the Team Check-in, and Entering a one-on-one Conversation as an Ally.

The one-on-one Check-in Message: How Are You Doing Today?

This can be done over text, Slack, or email if you are anxious about first having this conversation in-person or worried too much time will pass before you can connect live. "Mita, I wanted to let you know you have been on mind. How are you doing today? I saw the news of xyz and can't begin to imagine the kind of pain you might be experiencing right now. I am at a loss for finding the right words. Please let me know if I can do anything to support you. The team will be here to cover you if you need to take some time to disconnect from work. My calendar is open if you need anything."

The Team Check-in

This messaging can be used again in a Slack channel, an email, or a group text. You can also start a team meeting live with a similar message as well. "Hi everyone. I couldn't start the day (or this meeting) without acknowledging what so many are watching in our social media feeds: the news of xyz. I am at a loss for exactly what to say. I can't begin to imagine the pain some of you may be feeling, particularly those who belong to (insert community). Please know we are here to cover and support each other if you need to take time off, and my calendar is always open. I hope we continue to show up with kindness and empathy as we always strive to do for each other."

What Does it Mean to be an Ally?

An ally is someone who supports and advocates for other people who are part of a group or community that is treated unfairly, has harm or hurt inflicted upon them. The ally is generally not part of the community they are advocating for, because they use their privilege and power to help those who have been harmed. When we think of the process of being an ally, this is a lifelong commitment and process. This does not happen overnight. It's a continual investment in time and support.

I am on a journey to be an ally to many communities, including the Black community. I use the word "journey" because there is no destination I am trying to reach. The only people who can say, "Yes, Mita is an ally for the Black Community," are my Black friends and colleagues. My job is to build trust with my Black friends and colleagues, hold myself accountable, educate myself, and be consistent. My words must match my action, my intent match my impact. My job is not to be self-serving, center the conversation on me, and proudly call myself an ally. I will continue to make mistakes. I show up to apologize and do better and be better. I self-reflect on how I can approach the work of allyship differently. I recognize there can be a cost to allyship. I will give up comfort and pride to do this work. Finally, remember that each and every one of us can be an ally for someone at work. Checking in on those who have been harmed or hurt at work is an important first step.

Entering a one-on-one Conversation as an Ally

Entering a one-on-one conversation as someone on their journey to be an ally can be uncomfortable if you have never done this before. We need to be open to having these conversations. We need to force ourselves to accept the discomfort we may feel, understanding our discomfort as an ally cannot be more important than the pain or trauma a colleague may be experiencing. In these conversations, you may check-in on a colleague who is open to sharing with you. Or a colleague may come to you to directly to share an experience they have had. How we show up in these conversations matters.

As a Brown woman and a DEI leader, I continue to be on a journey to be an ally to the Black community. I continue to make mistakes, wondering if I am saying the right thing, or doing the wrong thing. And I have to remember that this isn't about me and centering how I feel: it's about the other person I am trying to hold space for in this conversation. Here's a framework I focus on, and the five things I remind myself as I enter into a conversation striving to be an ally:

1. **Please just listen. Allow the space for stories to be shared.**

   In a world that won't shut up, it's hard for us to just be present and listen because we want to talk and talk and talk. We just need to listen. Deeply listen to what is being shared and seek to understand. Either you have invited them to share, or they have approached you wanting to share something with you. Either way, they trust you to listen. They might be emotional. They may get quiet. Sit in the silence and emotion with them. It's okay to embrace the moments of quiet and not respond in the moment.

   When I check-in on my Black friends and colleagues, some want to share how they are feeling. Others do not. It's never my place or my job to force individuals to share anything. Pain and trauma can be deep. The important first step is that you checked in. They feel seen and valued by you.

2. **Please don't minimize their experience.**

"Are you sure that happened? Maybe you misunderstood what she said? Mita is one of the nicest people I have ever met."

"No way that happened! You must be joking?"

"Perhaps you are making this a bigger deal than it really is."

Please do not ask questions. Please do not make statements or question the validity of what is being shared. Or make it seem like they are unnecessarily venting. Now is not the time to be an investigative journalist, asking who, where, when, and why. Accept what they are telling you to be true. Because they are sharing their truth. Seek to understand and learn from what they are sharing.

3. **Please don't insert your own experiences.**

Please don't start telling stories about sexist or racist or homophobic experiences you have had in response to what they shared. After 9/11, it was the first time in my life I started to fear authority. I feared for my brother and my father and all the South Asian men in my life who could, for no reason, be dragged away and deemed a terrorist threat by police. My Black friends reminded me that this was the fear they have lived with all their lives. Remember, now is not the time to compare and contrast experiences in an attempt to show you understand their pain. Don't create a false equivalency, incorrectly assuming your experience and their experience are the same, even if superficially they may seem to share the same characteristics.

When there are long periods of silence, and someone is emotional during a conversation, our instinct can be to fill up the air to make it less uncomfortable. I try to stay present, ensure the person sees my eye contact. If this is an in-person conversation and I know the person well, I offer a tissue or lightly extend my hand on their hand or shoulder to show I am there for them.

I avoid phrases like "It's going to be okay" or "It will get better" or "Progress takes time."

Instead, I focus on phrases like:

- I am here for whatever you need.
- I am here to listen, there's no rush, please take your time.
- I can't imagine how painful this is for you. Thank you for trusting me and sharing.

4. Please don't try to problem-solve.

As leaders, we are trained to problem solve. The most difficult part about conversations, where someone is sharing with you racial trauma they have experienced, is the non-closure. You have left the conversation feeling like you couldn't help; you didn't brainstorm an action plan; you didn't provide a solution. It was a failed conversation. If ending institutional racism was so easy, we would have collectively eliminated it long ago. So our work is not done in one conversation. Our job is to keep engaging and not avoid these conversations.

5. Please do continue to educate yourself.

When ending the conversation, I thank the person for trusting me to have the conversation. I assure them that I am here for future conversations and that I will continue to educate myself. Please ask them how you can continue to be there for them. This might be a one-time conversation; the person may not want to connect and speak again. This also might be an opportunity to further develop a relationship and continue to engage with each other.

Finally, as someone who is on her journey to be an ally to the Black community, I remind myself of this: It is not the job of my Black friend or colleague to educate me. I cannot place this emotional burden on them. There is so much content out there to start educating myself as an ally. I don't always need to speak to a primary source, the person who is directly experiencing the pain, to learn about a lived experience that is not my own. And if I can Google the latest Tortilla Wrap Hack, the best beach properties in North Carolina, or how to properly sew on a button, I can rely on Google and other sources to help educate me.

Over time, as you get to better know and understand the colleagues you work with, this will become part of how you show up as an inclusive leader. You won't always have to be the one checking in or to initiate conversations. They, in return, will share with you what they are struggling with. Because you have built a foundation for trust and mutual understanding. You will inspire other leaders to show up in the moments that matter. And you will start to recognize that as we reimagine the idea of inclusion, we accept that it means sacrificing our own comfort to ensure others feel seen and heard.

Tips on Checking In on Colleagues Experiencing Trauma

- Please don't rely on your Employee Resource Groups (ERGs) to do this hard work; we as leaders must step up when it comes to allyship. Remember that your ERGs are not your DEI strategy.
- Please do not put pain on display. Checking in on colleagues is best done one-on-one. There may be a case when colleagues from an ERG approach you and ask you to help them create

(continued)

an event or conversation around the pain their community is experiencing. This must be done with much thought and care in partnership and close collaboration with the ERG.

- When having one-on-one check-ins, please just listen. Allow the space for stories to be shared.
- Please don't minimize their experience.
- Please don't insert your own experiences.
- Please don't push for them to share more.
- Please don't try to problem-solve.
- Please respect if they don't want to continue to share or they don't reach out again.
- Please don't ask that they reach out to other leaders to share their experiences. Remember, each time they share their experience, they may be reliving the trauma. And this trauma can also be intergenerational trauma, and something that has not been experienced just by them, but also their family members for generations.
- Please continue to educate yourself.
- Please remember your comfort is not more important than the pain and suffering they are experiencing.

4

I'm All for Diverse Talent. As Long as They Are Good.

"I'm all for diverse talent," this leader who oversaw one of our biggest clients explained. "As long as they are good."

Taking a deep breath and hoping to coax him into some self-reflection, I asked, "Can you share more about what you mean by 'as long as they are good'?"

"Listen, I am all for meeting talent," he continued, ignoring my question. "Happy to meet the internal candidate who is interested in the role. He is colored, right?"

My heart dropped. My throat went dry. I looked past him to see one of his team members standing behind him. She heard what he said and stared at me, her mouth hanging wide open.

"We don't use that term, colored, to describe anyone, today," I try to calmly explain, worried my voice was shaking. "We say people of color, and in this case . . ."

"Why not? Why can't I say that?" he interrupted me.

"Well," I said pausing. "It's an offensive, hurtful term dating back to the Jim Crow era, and racial segregation in the United States. We don't use it because . . ."

"How should I refer to him?"

"We should always ask people how they identify before making assumptions and never . . ."

"Okay, okay, okay I won't use that term," he said interrupting me again. "You know I'm Canadian, so I had no idea," he laughed, shrugged his shoulders, and walked away.

Several years ago, I was coaching a white leader as roles opened up on his team, consisting of all white leaders. Those openings were an opportunity to start to change the composition of his team. (And also to help him understand that the language he uses matters. He couldn't keep using "But I am Canadian" to absolve him of whatever he said.)

What this leader said aloud is the tension many leaders wrestle with quietly: they aspire to have a diverse workforce. Many accept that diverse teams perform better. They will proclaim they are focused on diversifying their teams. They are committed to diversity. But they don't want to sacrifice the quality of talent. They don't want to drop their standards, accept quotas, and hire someone just because they are "Black, Hispanic or Latino, or Asian." And so this is the myth we must debunk in order to begin to transform our workplaces: hiring and developing diverse talent, as long as they are good.

Do You Believe There Is a Limited Pool of Black Talent to Recruit From?

In 2020, Charlie Scharf joined a list of executives who revealed that they have more work to do on their DEI journey. The Wells Fargo CEO shared his views on the lack of representation at the bank, citing that there was "a very limited pool of Black talent to recruit from." Scharf later issued an apology after swift media backlash, stating that it was "an insensitive comment reflecting my own unconscious bias."[1]

In my time coaching leaders, I have heard a number of these phrases and more:

- There just aren't enough qualified Black candidates out there.
- It's not our issue, it's a pipeline issue.
- Of course, I want more people of color on my team. Recruiting can't find any candidates.

No matter what the wording is, it boils down to this: the underlying assumption that we lower the bar for "diverse talent." Because we don't believe or know or have seen "enough talented people of color" in the marketplace.

When I was once working with a South Asian leader, he said to me, "You know we brought in interns from Historically Black Colleges, we had a program," providing evidence that he cared about diversity. "But they just weren't as good as the other interns. We had to stop going there for interns."

"How many interns did you hire?" I had asked.

"Three."

You might find these examples uncomfortable or not believable. And if we are honest, others have heard these stories in our workplaces before. And even believed or continue to believe these myths ourselves.

So let's self-reflect and answer the following:

- Have you ever thought that focusing on "nondiverse talent" or white talent is lowering the bar for your team?
- Would you ever stop a partnership with a college because a handful of white interns from that college weren't very good?

- Do you believe there is a pipeline problem when it comes to white talent?
- As you think about your career, how many white individuals have you hired or referred for roles?
- Can you recall a time you worked with a white colleague who wasn't a fit or wasn't qualified to do the role? Has that made you more hesitant to hire white people over time?

Now let's self-reflect and answer the following:

- Have you ever thought that focusing on "diverse talent" is lowering the bar for your team?
- Would you ever stop a partnership with a Historical Black College or University because a handful of Black interns from that college weren't very good?
- As you think about your career, how many people of color have you hired or referred for roles?
- Do you believe there is a pipeline problem when it comes to people of color? Do you believe there is a pipeline problem for Black talent? Hispanic or Latino talent? Asian talent?
- Can you recall a time you worked with a Black colleague who wasn't a fit or wasn't qualified to do the role? Has that made you more hesitant to hire Black people over time? (You can also re-ask the question naming a specific community of color.)

So if you believe the myth that you can't hire "diverse talent" without lowering the bar, you won't make much progress on diversifying your workforce. Because very few people will fit whatever standards you have set in your head. If you hire a person of color and treat them like you did them a favor or they were a quota, they won't stay. Because as we discussed earlier, if you don't show up as an inclusive leader, you won't be able to retain them.

It's Time to Bust the Pipeline Myth

An underlying assumption in this myth: "I'm all for diverse talent. As long as they are good" is that there isn't "qualified" talent who identify as people of color. The pipeline just isn't there.

When I once worked with a leader in Vermont, they wanted to hire a head of market research. It was an opportunity to change the composition of a mostly white team. And yet they wanted to provide no relocation support, offering an average compensation package versus the market, including that the role had to be in state. And Vermont remains the second whitest state in the United States, 89.8 percent white.[2]

"It's a pipeline problem," proclaimed the leader. "We aren't getting any diverse slates from recruiting, there's nothing I can do about it." In this case, the leader failed to recognize what many of us do: we are responsible for "the pipeline problem" myth. We can create barriers that don't allow fair and equitable access to our roles. We can perpetuate the pipeline problem by setting up internal hurdles and criteria. We can use credentialing and degrees as a way to gatekeep who is worthy of consideration. Mirrortocracies, a term recently coined in place of meritocracies, are organizations where leaders hire individuals who remind them of themselves, versus hiring the best talent for the role. So in the Vermont example, attracting people of color candidates for this role was unrealistic. In the end, they hired a white candidate.

Finally, when we think of the "availability of talent," dynamics in the marketplace continue to shift. With the continued rise of remote work, you have access to talent across the globe and no longer need to hire with a specific location in mind. Prior to Elon Musk acquiring Twitter, the company's "work from anywhere" policy was an example of broadening access to talent and their commitment to diversifying their workforce. And their policy was having an impact; Twitter reported 9.4 percent Black representation in 2021 (vs. 6.9 percent the prior year) and 8 percent Hispanic/Latinx representation (Twitter uses the term Latinx instead of Latino) in 2021 (vs. 5.5 percent in 2020).[3]

"In an all-virtual environment there are very few limitations to where we can show up to meet talent as a company," James Loduca, then Twitter's vice president of inclusion, diversity, equity, and accessibility, told Bloomberg News. "We were able to hire folks in markets that we know have high populations of Black talent, markets that we know have high populations of Latinx talent."[4]

PwC is Tackling Workplace Equity by Supporting Black, Latinx Students

According to a Kaufman Fellow Report, the number of Black and Hispanic and Latino (PwC used the term Latinx) professionals with master's degrees increased by 133 percent and 400 percent, respectively, between 1980 and 2016. One of the study's key takeaways: "Latinx and Black students have been earning bachelor's and master's degrees at record rates, but those gains are not translating into representation."

Professional services firm PwC launched "Access Your Potential" as a way to create equal opportunity for students. According to the Higher Education Statistics agency, 5.5 percent of Black graduates are unemployed a year after they graduate, compared to 2.8 percent of white graduates. For those who do find work after graduating, only 53 percent of Black graduates secure full-time roles compared to 62 percent of white graduates. PwC expanded the Access Your Potential program to create new opportunities for 25,000 college-aged Black and Hispanic/Latinx students with a $125 million investment, looking to support those who struggle with landing full-time work after graduating.[5]

When we focus on myths like "diverse talent just isn't as good" or "there's a pipeline problem," it distracts us from the work we need to do. We need to focus on the role we can play in creating inclusive processes and hold ourselves accountable to finding the best talent for the role. While your recruiting organization has expertise and experience in this space, we must accept the responsibility that we as leaders have in hiring talent. In my time working with leaders, many are quick to put the responsibility on recruiting for diversifying their teams. Remember that this work belongs to all of us.

Remember That Language Matters

Before we discuss the ways in which you can personally impact how your organization recruits, let's stop for a moment to discuss language. On this work to transform our workplaces and make them more inclusive, language matters. On our journey to be more inclusive leaders, what we say, the words we choose, and how we express ourselves matter.

The hard work of building inclusive cultures comes down to the conversations happening every day in boardrooms, in virtual team meetings, and in one-on-one interactions. The words and phrases we use can reflect whether we are committed to the work for the long term, or whether we are checking the box and looking for quick fixes. Our words have significant impact on our colleagues whether or not we realize it.

And language is constantly changing. The terms we might use today we may no longer use tomorrow. As leaders we must have humility to evolve how we speak and how we approach being an inclusive leader.

Here are three simple rules I try to follow:

1. I strive to use inclusive language to respect everyone I interact with. I do my best not to misrepresent or stereotype others or make anyone feel marginalized. When I make mistakes, I apologize and own the harm I have caused. I listen and learn to educate myself, so I don't repeat causing harm.

2. I avoid acronyms and terms I don't understand. I try to avoid the trap of "well I heard someone else say that phrase so I'll say it too." Remember that Google is your friend. Take the time to learn words or phrases you don't understand.

3. I ask for help when I don't know or am unsure. For example, I never assume how someone identifies based on how they look or appear. I always ask, "How do you identity?" And I offer "I identify as a woman of color" to open the door for them to share how they identify.

When I coach leaders on language, I provide the background and history of terms. I offer other language they should use instead. And remember, there are some words that are considered incredibly harmful and hurtful that should no longer ever be used. My intent is to never shame or blame, but to educate and explain the context of why the term is hurtful to others.

As someone on a journey to be an ally to the Hispanic and Latino community, I have struggled with what terms to use. "To be considered Latina/Latino/Latinx, you or your ancestors must have come from a Latin American country: Mexico, Dominican Republic, Puerto Rico, Cuba, French-speaking Caribbean nations, Central or South America (though English-speaking regions)," David Bowles, professor at the University of Texas Río Grande Valley, told Oprah Daily.

"People who live in or are descended from a Spanish-speaking culture can define themselves as Hispanic. This includes people from or descended from Spain—but Spain is part of Europe, and thus not part of Latin America. Therefore, Spanish people could be described as Hispanic, but not Latino/Latina/Latinx," Dr. Luisa Ortiz Pérez, Executive Director of Vita-Activa.org, told Oprah Daily.[6]

And finally, the Merriam-Webster dictionary defines the term Latinx as being "originally formed as a word for those of Latin American descent who do not identify as being of the male or female gender or who simply don't want to be identified by gender."[7]

You will notice I have chosen to use the terms Hispanic and Latino in this book. In asking a number of friends and colleagues, they don't prefer the term Latinx and find it offensive. And they are not alone. According to the Pew Center for Research, only 3 percent of those who identify as Hispanic use the term Latinx to describe themselves.[8] When it comes to language, do your research. And as we discussed, when in doubt always ask those who you have built trusting and meaningful relationships for guidance.

Language Matters When It Comes to Attracting Talent

In my time coaching leaders, I often see inappropriate or hurtful language used when referring to how an organization attracts talent. Here are three commonly used phrases I recommend we stop using and offer language to use instead:

Instead of "Diverse Hire, Diversity Hire, or Diverse Talent," Use "Building Diverse Pipelines, Diverse Slates, Diverse Succession Plans"

Using the words diverse hire (diversity hire, or diverse talent) can have a damaging impact on your DEI efforts. Diverse hire implies that the only reason an individual was hired is because of a specific dimension of diversity. That they were hired because they were diverse, not because they were qualified.

Instead, focus your language around building diverse pipelines, and ensure you have diverse slates for roles. As a woman of color, I don't want to be labeled as a diverse hire. I want to be known for my experience, my talent, my expertise I bring to the organization.

(continued)

(*continued*)

Instead of: "Underrepresented Minorities," Use "Historically Marginalized Communities"

Using the term underrepresented minorities (URM) has become increasingly popular as companies look to diversify their workforce. URM references the low participation rates of ethnic and racial communities in fields and industries relative to their representation in the U.S. population.[9] Unfortunately, when we use this term, we don't acknowledge that these communities have been systemically and historically excluded. By using only this one umbrella term, we also erase the differences of individuals in this group.

Instead of using URM, consider using the phrase historically marginalized communities. By using this language, you are acknowledging that there are communities who have systematically been denied access to economic, political, and cultural participation. I also use people of color more broadly and interchangeably with historically marginalized communities when speaking with leaders who might not yet understand the term historically marginalized communities. And aren't ready to use it.

You can also be specific about what communities you are referencing and wanting to serve, for example, Black/African-American,[10] Hispanic or Latino,[11] or Native American/American Indian/Indigenous American.[12] Often, it's important to be specific to ensure you are honoring a community's history and their voices.

Instead of "Diversity of Thought" Use "Diversity of Representation"

Increasingly, diversity of thought has become a popular phrase to express what we believe to be the intent of our DEI efforts.

By only embracing diversity of thought, we aren't having uncomfortable conversations when it comes to gender and racial inequities in our organizations. We aren't specifically talking about whose voice is missing from the table and why.

Instead of using just diversity of thought, use the language that "diversity of thought doesn't happen without diversity of representation." You can also use the phrase, "focusing on diversity of representation" when referring to what you hope to achieve through your DEI efforts, particularly in recruiting.

Finally, Here's How We Can Partner with Recruiting to Make Impact

As we reflect on how we attract talent, consider the following three questions on how we can partner with recruiting to make impact:

1. How Can You Get Access to Diverse Pipelines?

Build Partnerships for the Long Term Instead of evoking "the pipeline problem" or blaming recruiting, it's our responsibility as leaders to partner with organizations that have access to diverse pipelines. In my time working with supply chain leaders, we built a strong partnership with the National Society of Black Engineers (NSBE). Ahead of their annual conference, I asked the head of supply chain to contribute funding along with what I had available in my DEI budget. He sent team members to the conference along with recruiters. I set expectations the first year we attended a NSBE conference: "We are looking to build a long-term partnership, not just make a few quick hires." I was pleasantly surprised that first year when we did make two hires. We built a five-year partnership over time, contributing a bit more money each year, providing more resources, and ultimately hiring over 50 individuals during the course of the partnership.

The head of supply chain and his team became personally invested in this partnership.

As we discussed earlier, just like when building any relationship, this takes time, commitment, and trust. Do the research and partner with recruiting to widen your pool of prospective candidates for your industry. Ask organizations what their needs are. Help fund and attend conferences, offer workshops, be a panelist, and take the time to meet talent in person or virtually.

In larger organizations with more budget, you can advocate to hire diversity sourcers. Building your organization's employer brand with historically marginalized communities doesn't happen overnight. Invest in hiring diversity sourcers who report to recruiting and have a dotted line to your chief diversity officer. They will identify the right key partnerships and build these ongoing relationships, helping to build a diverse pipeline for your organization. They will help hiring managers craft inclusive job descriptions and interview questions that are non-biased, consistent, and ultimately creating an inclusive candidate experience. Finally, diversity sourcers can analyze your recruiting data to find the gaps in hiring talent from historically marginalized communities. And while your recruiting team may already be doing some of this, having diversity sourcers helps drive focus around this and can have significant impact on reviewing questions like these:

1. Are your partnerships helping attract more candidates from historically marginalized communities at the top of the funnel?
2. How do you define a diverse slate? Are you able to achieve diverse slates for most of your roles?
3. How do you define a diverse interview panel? Are you able to achieve diverse interview panels? Who is selected to interview and why?
4. Do you notice patterns for roles on where candidates from specific communities didn't advance to the next interview stage?

And for more senior roles, if you hire an executive search firm, ask them the above and hold them accountable.

What's a Diverse Slate?

A diverse slate is a part of your talent strategy where from the start, and with intention, you search for candidates who identify as belonging to different communities. As you kick off the hiring process, ask your recruiter how your organization defines a diverse slate. If you don't do this, now's the time to start.

The term diverse slate originates from the National Football League's implementation of the Rooney Rule in 2003. This was an effort to increase the diversity of representation amongst the coaching staff, where hiring managers were required to interview at least one individual from a historically marginalized community.[13]

Here's an example of how a company may define a diverse slate. The hiring manager interviews a final slate of five candidates, including one candidate who is a woman and one who is a person of color. According to research in *Harvard Business Review*, when you only have one person of color on a slate, they have very little chance of being hired. The research showed that the "two in pool effect" helps DEI efforts; when there are at least two women candidates on the final slate, the odds of hiring a woman candidate are 79 time greater. If there are two candidates of color on the final slate, the odds of hiring them are 194 times greater.[14]

Finally, ensure you have positive intent behind your goal to achieve diverse slates. Former Miami Dolphins head coach Brian Flores is suing the NFL, alleging the Denver Broncos and New York Giants held what he termed "sham interviews" and

(continued)

(*continued*)

were simply "diversity window dressing."[15] Wells Fargo was also accused of having fake job interviews, interviewing a woman or a person of color, even though the job had already been promised to someone else. So on paper they could document achieving "diverse slates."[16] Before embarking on trying to achieve diverse slates, make sure you educate your teams on the intent behind it.

Rethink Employee Referrals I once worked with two co-founders who were frustrated with their internship program.

"We worked so hard," they both lamented. "And on the first day, 12 white women showed up. How could that happen?"

"How did you recruit for interns?" I asked.

"We had every employee in the company blast their networks. We invested so much time in finding these interns."

Unfortunately, employee referral initiatives can do more harm than good when it comes to our DEI efforts. People tend to refer people like themselves. For example, let's say you have a majority white leadership team, and you have an opening on that team. You rely solely on their referrals to fill the role. If the leaders' networks are not diverse, they will end up referring other white leaders. In a number of instances, I have coached leaders to pause employee referrals completely. If you continue to push for employee referrals, make sure to communicate you are targeting diverse slates for roles.

Be a Talent Scout We all need to be talent scouts. It's not just recruiting's job to find talent. Attend virtual and live conferences affiliated with your industry. Volunteer to speak about your career journey.

Connect with talent you meet and stay in touch on LinkedIn even if there is no job opening. Be open to remote work; meet individuals in other locations. Build and expand your network by checking in over virtual connects and keeping them top of mind for future roles. Your personal investment as a talent scout is critical to see the change in representation in your organization.

2. How Can You Help Create Fair and Inclusive Interviewing Experiences?

Adhere to the Same Process for All Candidates   Ensure you outline the interview stages. Finalize the slate of interviewers who interview all selected candidates. Align on the questions all candidates will be asked.

Why is this important? Consider the following two interview scenarios:

- You feel a connection from the beginning. You both grew up in the same town and both played lacrosse at Stanford. You don't ask substantive questions. You shorten the process for them, recommending they get an offer.
- You feel uncomfortable from the beginning. They don't seem as qualified and wouldn't be a cultural fit (more on that concept shortly). You ask that they be interviewed by more people; you feel uncertain about their candidacy.

No matter what the scenario, adhere to a consistent process to minimize bias, which leads to better outcomes.

Take Detailed Notes   Let the candidate know you are taking notes. If interviewing virtually, tools like BrightHire can record your interview. That way you can rewatch later, staying focused during the actual interview. Detailed notes are important to ensure you are assessing candidates fairly and minimizing bias. Without detailed notes to review after the interview, we can fall prey to a number of biases on why we may like or dislike a candidate.

Submit an Interview Evaluation in a Timely Manner   Schedule time after the interview to complete your evaluation. Target to complete this within 24 hours. This is critical so your memory of the conversation is fresh, and you can understand the notes you took during the interview. The more time that passes, the more distractions will take over and the less likely you will be to remember the details of the interview. This is when bias can creep in.

3. How Do We Evaluate Talent?

"They wouldn't be a fit," a senior leader says. "They wouldn't fit with our culture."

I can't recall how many times I have heard this feedback as leaders evaluate talent. Not a cultural fit. Just wouldn't fit in with the team. Don't see them getting along with everyone else. These feelings can arise particularly if the candidate doesn't look like, act like, or think like the leader.

Cultural fit has increasingly become dangerous code language. The lack of cultural fit is an acceptable way to reject candidates. Because no one wants to be responsible for a bad hire, we move on to the next candidate. One that will be a cultural fit.

But how do we define our work cultures? It's the values, behaviors, and sometimes unspoken and unwritten rules of how we operate. Don't leave culture as a vague term that's up to interpretation. Be specific on what makes up your culture and what qualities will make individuals successful in your organizations.

When evaluating talent, start with these three principles to help minimize bias:

Discourage Questions That Are Synonymous with Cultural Fit Leaders might stop using the words cultural fit. But that doesn't stop them from asking a host of questions that come back to the same vague principle. Watch out for:

- Could I travel with this person to client meetings?
- How can I assess our chemistry over video?
- Could I enjoy a glass of wine with them?
- Would I invite them to my home for dinner?

When you hear variations of these questions, go back to the job description. Evaluate talent on a skills fit and a values fits.

Focus on Skills Fit What are the skills needed to do this job successfully? What are the prior experiences that would enable them to make an impact here? What have they learned from the mistakes they have made and how do they continue to up-skill themselves? No one individual will check all the boxes for the skills you are looking for. Remember, you want talent who will learn and grow with the organization.

Define Your Values, Then Evaluate for Values Fit Ensure your organization's values are well defined. Because you can't assess for a values fit if you don't have defined values. Some key examples:

- Starbucks key value: Acting with courage, challenging the status quo, and finding new ways to grow our company and with each other.[17]

  Interview question: Tell me about a time you had to lead with courage and conviction to challenge the status quo.
- Google key value: Faster is better than slow.[18]

  Interview question: Can you reflect on a time you brought a product to market and how that process could have been faster?

- Whole Foods key value: We promote team member growth and happiness.[19]

    Interview question: How have you role modeled focusing on your own mental health for your teams?

When you are clear about what skills and experiences you are looking for, and the values that matter, it becomes easier to evaluate talent fairly and consistently.

Remember, it's easy to blame processes and structures that are broken, especially when it comes to how we hire talent. It's harder to acknowledge that we each play a critical role in knowingly or unknowingly deciding who is "worthy" of joining our organizations. If each of us work to make the hiring process more inclusive, we can have a ripple effect across our teams and the organization and inspire others to model and adopt our behaviors.

Tips for Leaders on Focusing on Increasing Diversity of Representation in Their Organizations

- Self-reflect on why you may doubt that talent from historically marginalized communities might not be as good.
- Bust the pipeline myth when you hear others bring it up as a way to justify not being able to attract talent from historically marginalized communities.
- Remember that language matters; part of the work of being inclusive leaders is to educate ourselves on what words we choose to use.
- Accept that you will make mistakes when it comes to language; apologize, educate yourself, and move forward.

- Consider the ways in which you can partner with recruiting, including investing in access to diverse pipelines, rethinking employee referrals, and being a talent scout.
- Take responsibility for how you can minimize bias by helping to create fair and inclusive interviewing processes.
- Finally, challenge the idea of cultural fit. Ensure it doesn't become a way to rule out candidates who don't look like, act like, or think like you or the majority of your employee population.

We Protect the A-holes Because Our Businesses Wouldn't Run Without Them.

"What? He's staying?" I said incredulously. I couldn't believe he was staying. It seemed impossible to me.

"Yes," the Human Resources colleague blurted out. "One of the leaders intervened on his behalf," he confessed to me over lunch. "I was surprised as well. Apparently, the business can't run without him."

Early in my career, I had a colleague confide in me regarding a group work email they had received. Another colleague had taken a picture of one of the vice presidents, who was a white leader, hugging a Black colleague at a team event, without their knowledge. This colleague then went on to email the picture with the following message to a number of team members: #ThisVPLovesDarkMeat

At the time, the mid-sized company we worked for had a clear and detailed process when it came to reporting harassment and bullying: a 1-800 number where you could call to report anonymously and also a specific email address; a zero-tolerance policy on creating an environment where all were respected; a business integrity team that oversaw what was being reported; a thorough investigation process; yearly mandated all-day anti-harassment and bullying training. On paper, it was one of the best-in-class processes set up to protect "the inclusive culture" so many of us were working hard to build.

The colleague who had reached out to me about the email was a person of color; they had been included in this group work email message consisting mostly of white colleagues. They were stunned and horrified that their white colleague could send something like this. I encouraged them and supported them in reporting the incident. This clearly went against our detailed code of conduct and was a fireable offense; there was digital evidence and a number of witnesses. It also was not something said or done accidentally. It was not something they could deny or have no memory of. This person took a picture, created a message for the picture, and then emailed it to a group of colleagues. It was premeditated.

But despite the elaborate and detailed process this company had created to protect its culture, and its people, that colleague was never fired. One of the leaders who sat on the business integrity team intervened on his behalf. The business apparently couldn't run without this individual's technical expertise. The leader saved his job. So the colleague only received a written warning for his behavior. And apparently this was not his first "written warning." I later heard he then went back to his team to reprimand them and exclaimed, "I can't believe you all can't take a joke. I mean this went up to the

Business Integrity Committee. Thank God I have friends in high places, otherwise you would have ruined my career."

In my time working with companies and leaders, I have realized this: It's not always the processes and systems that fail us. It's us. We fail us. Because often we fail to follow the rules, the standards, the processes we set up as checks and balances for us all.

In the example I shared, here are three key take-aways:

1. Despite a sophisticated and detailed process for reporting bullying and harassment, someone in power intervened on this colleague's behalf and chose not to follow the rules set forth. The other leaders on this Business Integrity Committee also ultimately agreed with the decision to only give him a written warning.

2. This was not the first time this colleague had done something inappropriate at work. Despite a sophisticated and detailed process, exceptions were for certain individuals. Sometimes those individuals hold some type of privilege that gives them the "benefit of the doubt." They have more room to make mistakes and they are given more chances. They may also be perceived as being more "integral" to the business than others.

3. Finally, the only person to report this was a person of color. The other white colleagues on the email chain didn't say anything. Either because they didn't find it offensive, didn't think it was their place to get involved, or just weren't sure what to say or do. For any of the white colleagues, this could have been a moment they showed up as an ally. Instead, they chose to stay silent. And yes, let's remember that being silent is a choice.

We often fail to recognize that inclusive cultures can't survive without inclusive leaders who stand up for what is right. Standing up for what is right means you are willing to take action against what you absolutely will not tolerate in your organization. And if individuals have a pattern of hurting or harming others in our workplaces, we need to ensure they leave our organization and move on to their next chapter.

In my time coaching leaders, I have watched too many leaders fall into this trap: protecting and allowing an individual to continue to work in their organization who has a pattern of hurting and harming others. Leaders will do so at the expense of losing other employees. They will do so at the expense of losing the trust of their teams. And they will do so at the expense of even damaging their own leadership brand.

"I've known Mita for years. People just misinterpret her sense of humor."

"Don't worry about it. He will retire soon."

"She grew up in a different time and place."

"They are just an asshole; you need to get over it and stop being so sensitive."

"Because sure, he might be an a-hole, but the business, well it just can't run without him."

The question then becomes: How far will we go to protect those who are destroying our culture?

Why Can't We Say Goodbye to Toxic Leaders?

Why can't we just let go, move on, and say goodbye to that one person, who is toxic, a bully, a jerk, an a-hole?

Here are questions I ask leaders to self-reflect on as they struggle with this decision:

- Why do I continue to allow Mita to stay in this organization? What is it about her, her skill set, and her experiences that make her irreplaceable?
- Do I accept the feedback others have about Mita? Do I dismiss, rationalize, or justify when I hear that she is behaving badly?

- What am I afraid will happen if Mita leaves? What would happen in the short term after she left? What would happen in the long term?
- Do I have a successor in mind to replace Mita? Can I work with HR and Recruiting to identify individuals who could take over her role?
- Have I listed out the good I believe Mita continues to do versus the harm she is inflicting upon the team and the rest of the company?
- In the time Mita has worked for me, how many people have moved off her team internally? How many people have left the company?
- Have I placed a greater importance on my personal friendship/ work relationship with Mita over the harm she is inflicting on our culture?
- Does continuing to protect Mita and allowing her to work here negatively or positively impact how people ultimately view me as a leader?

It's time to stop protecting the a-holes. The a-holes don't make up or define our company. We need to wake up and realize our people are the company. And our businesses cannot run without our people. It's our job to protect our people from the a-holes if we want to protect the inclusive cultures we are working so hard to build.

So how do we do this? Where do we start? Let's start by familiarizing ourselves with some key terms.

What Is Harassment?

According to the U.S. Equal Opportunity Commission (EEOC), harassment is a form of employment discrimination. Harassment is "unwelcome conduct that is based on race, color, religion, sex (including sexual orientation, gender identity, or pregnancy), national origin, older age (beginning at age 40), disability, or genetic information (including family medical history)."[1]

It becomes unlawful when it creates a hostile work environment; an environment that would be intimidating to reasonable people. This can be difficult to prove for the person who is the target of harassment. It can also be difficult for those of us trying to help and intervene to spot these behaviors.

Harassment can show up in many ways. First, in writing. This may be easier to spot: offensive jokes or comments, or derogatory messages sent over text, emails, Slacks, or written on a piece of paper. (An Asian American colleague once had a post-it on her office cubicle that said, "Go Back To Where You Came From.")

Next, in everyday conversation, this can be more difficult if there were no witnesses. It can become a dispute between the target and the perpetrator, even more so when the perpetrator may hold more power at work. If there are witnesses, they may not feel like it's their place to get involved or are too scared to speak up. With many virtual meetings now being recorded, there may be opportunities to sit back and watch what took place.

Third, when it comes to physical harassment, it can be more subtle in nature and less obvious. It can be someone standing too close to someone repeatedly on purpose. Touching a person or their clothing. (I had a colleague whose manager would "accidentally" yet repeatedly touch her hijab.) It can also include sexually suggestive hand gestures and facial expressions, either targeted at someone or they witness another colleague doing it. It can also include playing offensive and harmful music (I can recall a white colleague, standing directly outside of the office's main doors, singing loudly to music including saying the N word repeatedly.)

Finally, visual harassment is another type of behavior to be on the look out for. This includes having pictures of a sexual nature in common areas or in an office, watching or sharing pornographic or violent videos. (I recall a group of colleagues, during a break from a meeting, gathering around a laptop to watch the Paris Hilton and Rick Salomon sex tape video.)

This can be wearing clothing with offensive or harmful, hurtful, sexist, racist language. (I once had a colleague who thought it was funny to wear a racist Abercrombie & Fitch t-shirt to work on a "Throwback Thursday." The t-shirt read: "Wong Brothers Laundry Service—Two Wongs Can Make It White" depicting two Asian men as caricatures, with slanted eyes wearing cone-shaped hats.)[2]

What Is Bullying?

The website stopbullying.gov (managed by the U.S. Department of Health and Human Services) offers support for kids, and their parents, who are the targets of bullying. And what they describe happening on school yards also happens in our workplaces every single day. "Bullying is unwanted, aggressive behavior . . . that involves a real or perceived power imbalance."[3] While bullying and harassment can look the same, there's a distinction when it comes to our workplace policies and the law. The negative behavior exhibited by a bully elevates to harassment when the behavior targeted at an individual is also based on a protected class (as defined in the EEOC's harassment definition).

In a workplace, those who bully may be looking to solidify their power or gain more power. They may bully to get what they want. They may bully to make themselves feel more powerful than they actually are. And finally, they may have been bullied themselves at home or at work and decide to exhibit those same behaviors on to others.

And bullying can still thrive in a virtual world. Individuals can feel shunned or left out of virtual meetings. Bosses and coworkers can be peering past our cameras and listening to the soundtrack of our lives. Judgments are placed on how we look, where we are Zooming from, and how "professional" we appear.

Bullying behavior can happen one time or can be repetitive. In my experience coaching leaders, where there is smoke, there is fire. Someone who has bullied an individual has usually bullied others as well, and there is usually a pattern to their bullying behavior.

In the workplace, verbal and social bullying are the most common. This can happen in person, or in our virtual world showing up in texts, emails, or Slack messages. Verbal bullying can include teasing a colleague, giving them unwelcome nicknames, making inappropriate comments and jokes, or threatening to cause harm (for example, a manager repeatedly threatening to fire a team member).

Social bullying can involve intentionally attempting to damage someone's reputation at work or their relationships. This may include leaving someone out of meetings or events on purpose. Telling other colleagues not to associate with them. Spreading rumors about them at work. And embarrassing and shaming them publicly when they make mistakes, offer a different opinion, or when they ask a question the bully doesn't know the answer to.

Finally, gaslighting is another form of subtle bullying. It's psychological abuse where an individual tries to gain power and control over you by instilling self-doubt. As someone who has been the target of gaslighting in the workplace, I know firsthand how damaging it can be. You start thinking you are imagining things. You know you are being excluded and undermined. Your productivity decreases. Your confidence plummets.

How Prevalent is Workplace Bullying?

According to the U.S. Workplace Bullying Institute 2021 Survey, 30 percent of people have direct experience being bullied (up 57 percent from 2017); another 19 percent have witnessed it; 49 percent are affected by bullying. Other notable key findings:

■ Bullying remains to be tied to power in the workplace; 65 percent of bullies are bosses.

■ In our virtual world of work, bullying happens mostly in virtual meetings, not emails.

■ Men are the majority of bullies, 67 percent, and slight majority of targets, 51 percent.

■ The most frequently chosen "positive" employer reaction was zero-tolerance.

■ Accountability for bully is starting (23 percent believe this) with punishment, termination, quitting.[4]

As a leader, use your influence and power to ensure your organization has some of these best practices in place to continue to help build an inclusive culture. Because it's time to stop bullies from thriving in our organizations, let's:

Enact a Zero-Tolerance Policy

Zero-tolerance policies are rising in popularity at companies. They can hold employees as well as partners and suppliers accountable. However, according to the EEOC's antiharassment task force, "zero tolerance" policies can be misleading and counterproductive if they are not properly defined.[5]

If you have a zero-tolerance policy, share it broadly and consistently, and be specific on what it covers. This may include no weapons, drugs, or alcohol at work, or using pornographic materials. Outline some of the behaviors you will have zero tolerance for, including the following: the use of sexist, racist, and homophobic language, and threatening or intimidating others. Ensure you have a stance on behavior outside of work, including social media channels. In an always-on world, we are all ambassadors of our company, as evidenced by the firing of Amy Cooper by her employer Franklin Templeton after she was caught on video calling the police and making a false claim against Christian Cooper, a Black man who was bird watching in Central Park.[6]

Dismantle Your Performance Review Process

It's time to dismantle your performance review system. Make 360 feedback at the heart of how leaders are evaluated, tied to their compensation and impacting all career opportunities. Consider utilizing Korn Ferry's Leadership Assessment or Culture Amp's feedback tools to start. Each individual in the leader's department should give feedback. For bullies who are exceptional at managing up, this will provide a holistic view of their leadership. The feedback should be anonymous and delivered by a third-party coach along with the manager.

Depending on the behavior, leaders should have the opportunity to change and not be immediately "cancelled." However, the runway to change behavior needs to be well defined and within a specific time frame. You can consider hiring a coach for the leader who is accountable to their manager. Or ask the leader to take a leave of absence where they can seek anger management classes or therapy. If the behavior change doesn't occur, and if it's not sustained, they need to leave the organization.

Can We Help Toxic Leaders?

When people are hurt, they may lash out and hurt other people. Hurt people hurt people. Leaders who are bullies may have been bullied themselves. They likely have insecurities and have deep trauma they have never healed from, and they lash out at others. So can we help toxic leaders? Here are three things you and your organization can do, depending on the severity of the negative, hurtful, and harmful behavior they have displayed:

- **Ask the toxic leader to leave.** Give them detailed feedback on their behavior and let them know it's time for them to move on. Sometimes the damage they have done internally is too much to repair. Even if you try to support them in staying, their teams and peers may no longer trust them. Asking them to leave may be one of the best options and in the best interest of all parties involved for everyone to move forward and heal.
- **Provide a six-month leave of absence.** Offer them unpaid time off to understand the harm they have inflicted and to give them an opportunity to reflect and work on themselves. If they choose to come back, they have to share how they plan to show up differently at work. They must be willing to address with their teams how they have changed as a leader. If the toxic behavior continues, you must immediately exit them.
- **Mandate therapy, not coaching.** Finally, in my time working for, working with, and observing toxic leaders, "executive coaching" is rarely the answer. I have watched many a toxic leader be mandated to work with a coach, only to slip back into their old behaviors, without addressing the root cause of why they behave this way. Mandating therapy as a condition of continued employment is more likely to help this leader heal so they stop hurting others.

Address Conflicts of Interest

What if the leader who is bullying their team is the Chief Human Resources Officer (CHRO)? What if they are close friends with the organization's general counsel? What if they sit on the business integrity team and review all complaints? The leader who is accused of bullying cannot be involved in their own investigation. Place them on a leave of absence so they cannot influence or intimidate individuals as the investigation occurs.

Some forms of retaliation are clear during and after an investigation if the leader in question is part of the investigation or continues to interact with the person or people they are accused of bullying; facing job loss, being denied a pay increase, or a promotion. Other types of retaliation can be difficult to document, including being excluded from meetings, being denied access to leadership, or being removed from assignments. If the leader accused of bullying is on a leave of absence, a fair process for all involved is more assured.

Reimagine Your Investigation Process

It's time to invest and hire third-party investigators to conduct investigations. Individuals need expertise on how to conduct interviews. They must follow the investigation protocol, should understand employment laws for your state, and be able to work with legal counsel. Too often, HR business partners who conduct investigations have not been properly trained. If they haven't been trained properly, don't put them in a position to investigate and jeopardize the well-being of all of the parties involved.

When you have leaders investigating other leaders, it's difficult to have checks and balances. One time when I reported a leader's bullying incident, I was told "they are a major a-hole, you need to move past it." Internal employees didn't investigate in fear of this leader retaliating. So follow the example of companies like Uber, CBS, and Essence, who brought in law firms to help investigate claims of bullying, harassment, and inappropriate behavior in the workplace.

If you have a Code or Business Integrity Committee, consider nominating select employees from different functions and levels to serve. When I was an MBA student at Duke University, the institution's Code Committee included both professors and students who were nominated by our community. It created a shared responsibility by all to promote a climate of integrity. Ensure you share investigation themes with your leadership and your board to discuss appropriate interventions. Collaborate with your DEI team and legal team to provide additional training and support to the individuals and teams who have been impacted by this toxic behavior.

Treat Your Exit Interviews Like Customer Reviews

Our employees are our forgotten consumers. If we receive a customer complaint, we look to fix the issue immediately. If we receive a complaint during an exit interview, let's address it with the same sense of urgency.

Exit interviews are the most undervalued tool we have. Sometimes they are not done or are poorly documented. Employees may not be honest about their experiences. Start by ensuring them that standard questions are used for every exit interview. Ensure the interviewer is not the manager of the department employee and that they have been trained. Follow up with a short questionnaire to capture anything that was missed. Consider offering exit interviews several weeks after the employee has left, to give them time to collect their thoughts.

Share exit interview themes frequently with your leadership team and board. Hold leaders accountable for their attrition. If a leader has had five women of color resign from their team within the last month, start asking the tough questions. Attrition should be tied to their performance reviews. If enough people leave their team, it may be time for that leader to leave as well.

As a South Asian woman and a woman of color, I grew up and worked in a time where people who look like me haven't always been accepted and celebrated. As a child, I was bullied both verbally and physically by my peers.

The bullies thrived because no one stopped them; not the teachers, not the parents, and not law enforcement. They were born into an ecosystem that enabled their behavior. And no one warned me that those same schoolyard bullies would also be waiting for me in Corporate America.

I was "renamed" Mohammed because a manager couldn't pronounce my full name Madhumita and refused to call me Mita. I was once told that people liked me because I acted "white and assimilated well." I was once told I was incompetent and no one else would ever want me on their team. I was screamed at over and over again. I was once called a rat; I had my work questioned and undermined; I had my job threatened. And in each of those moments in my career, I wondered when I couldn't use my voice and speak up, why no one else around me stood up for me.

According to the U.S. Workplace Bullying Institute 2021 Survey, 66 percent of Americans are aware that workplace bullying happens.[7] Some don't feel comfortable saying anything. Some don't know what to say. Another common excuse I hear for leaders not intervening on behalf of someone who is being hurt or harmed at work: "It's not my place to get involved."

For decades harassment training led by Human Resources and Legal has focused on the perpetrator, the individual who is harassing and bullying others in the workplace. By the time an employee calls the code line, or reports an individual to legal, it may be too late: The matter has escalated to a point of no return. As employment lawyer Asha Santos shared in an interview with *Harvard Business Review:* "Many of the claims I see result because some behavior started out relatively minor and was allowed to grow. I call this a gateway behavior. When people look the other way during an incident of low-level harassment, it allows the harassment to intensify over time.

By intervening early, at the first sign of a red–flag moment, bystanders can break the cycle and prevent the problem from worsening."[8]

We each have a responsibility to protect the culture we have worked so hard to build, and we must all be empowered to act. When we see something, we cannot look the other way. We have a responsibility to say something. We have a responsibility to act.

When You See Something, Say Something

When you see something, say something. Focus on these six ways you can help:

Intervene in the Moment

Whether it's in a meeting or at a work event, being an effective ally for someone requires us to act. You can step in by helping to remove the person from the situation. You can do this without having to name the behavior directly in the moment, particularly if you are the more junior person in the room and the toxic leader happens to be a senior leader. Depending on how comfortable you are in the moment, you can interrupt the toxic leader, pull them aside, and say, "I don't know if you realize you are making Mita uncomfortable. Let's move on to another topic."

Intervene after the Incident Occurs

It's never too late to intervene. If you couldn't say something in the moment, find time to follow up with the leader who caused harmed. As we discussed before, this may be a good opportunity to educate them on intent versus impact. This may be the first time they have done or said something like that, and this is an opportunity to educate them. Or there may be a pattern of bullying that's well known in the organization. If you don't feel comfortable talking to the toxic leader directly, talk to another trusted individual in the organization to seek their advice. There might be another leader who can help intervene.

Check-in with Your Colleague

Check-in with the person who was targeted after the incident occurs. You may have been a witness; you may have heard something happened through others. Actively listen and show empathy. Remember that silence is okay. Ask them how you can help and what you can do for them now. If they are uncomfortable speaking about it with you, let them know you are always available to talk to them in the future.

Support Your Colleague in Reporting the Incident

Support your colleague in reporting what happened. This could be helping them understand how to report an incident in your organization, coming forward as a witness, attending the meeting with them to see Human Resources, or being available right before and right after they meet with Human Resources. If an investigation is started, they might feel anxious and scared and will need friends they can count on for support. All of these small acts of support show them that they are not alone.

Watch out for Retaliation

Watch out for retaliation. It may not occur immediately after the incident is reported. You can support your colleague in taking notes and document what's occurring, particularly if you are a witness. Encourage your colleague to also document what's happening and be ready to help them report the retaliation. Keeping notes is an important part of helping your colleague validate their own feelings and see if there are any patterns or trends to share back with HR.

Continue to Check-in on Your Colleague

Finally, continue to check-in on your colleague. If this person is repeatedly experiencing bullying or harassment at work, they will need your continued support. Particularly if the toxic leader is still there targeting them. They may need help moving to another team, transferring to a different part of the organization, or finding a new opportunity outside of the company.

It's time to stop bullies from thriving in our organizations. It means we must no longer hide behind the myth that we must protect the a-holes because our businesses wouldn't run without them. We are living in the Great Awakening, where employees will no longer work in organizations where they are not respected. They are waking up to the realization that they deserve better. They now demand to work in organizations where they are respected and supported, and where they feel they belong. Leaders must wake up to the fact that talent will no longer tolerate the behavior they once did. And it's time to start protecting our employees, because without them, there would be no company.

Tips on How to Protect Your People, and Not the A-holes

- Continue to self-reflect on why you or others may be protecting toxic leaders.
- Understand the difference between harassment and bullying; educate your colleagues on how this can show up in our workplaces.
- Educate yourself on your organization's existing policies when it comes to anti-harassment and bullying policies.
- Use your influence and power to ensure your organization has best practices in place including enacting a zero-tolerance policy, dismantling your performance review process, addressing conflicts of interest, reimagining your investigation process, and treating your exit interviews like customer reviews.

(continued)

- If you see something, say something. We all have a responsibility to protect the inclusive cultures we are working so hard to build.
- Remember that it's never too late to intervene.
- Check-in with colleagues impacted by harassment and bullying on how you can continue to help support them.

MYTH

6

Why Are You Asking for a Raise? You and Your Husband Make More Than Enough Money.

"Oh come on, Mita," a former manager chuckled. "Why are you asking for a raise? You and your husband make more than enough money!"

This was his immediate response when I asked for my compensation to be reviewed. I had researched and read every article on the topic of negotiating to prepare for asking for more money. **I knew my value:** I understood what others in roles similar to mine, both internally and externally, were earning. **I knew where my performance stood:** I had been consistently given high ratings during past performance reviews. Leaders across the organization all continued to vouch for my significant impact with feedback and testimonials.

I picked the best time to bring up the topic of my compensation: during my annual performance review conversation when I knew the company gave out merit-based increases and bonuses and reviewed overall salaries. **I practiced and practiced:** I showed up confident, positive, and smiling. Because I was uncomfortable talking about money, I needed to ensure I was being valued for my expertise and track record of success. Being valued meant being paid fairly.

When he asked the question, I was stunned into silence. I didn't know how to respond or what to say. In that moment, he made me feel ashamed for even asking. And I felt a surge of anger for being devalued. I felt a lump growing in my throat as he swiftly changed topics. Rewinding that scene in my head over and over again in the years since, I wish I had found the courage to reply: "Why does my husband's career have anything to do with how much you pay me?"

On our journey to reimagine what inclusion looks like, we must talk about money. So one of the myths we must debunk when it comes to closing the gender pay gap is this: White women and women of color don't negotiate. We need to take responsibility for contributing to the gender pay gap. We don't ask for more. We settle for and accept what we are given. We don't know our worth. We let others define our value.

But in fact, many of us do. We do negotiate and ask. And when we do try to advocate for ourselves, we can become the target of gaslighting. We are dismissed, minimized, and left alone to question ourselves, replaying the scenario over and over again in our minds. We are filled with self-doubt, wondering if we should have said anything in the first place.

We are met with "Why are you asking for a raise?" (The response from a former manager.) "I am surprised you are questioning the offer. This is a very fair offer." (The response from a former recruiter, who was surprised I was negotiating.) And "Oh, I thought you would do this for free since we went to the same graduate school and all." (The response from a former classmate who asked me to speak at a Fortune 500 company-wide event for free. It should also be noted that we weren't friends; they barely made eye contact with me during our two years in school.)

As I grew more savvy in my career, after having experienced more and more setbacks when it came to pay and watching women I knew have the same experience, I learned how to better play the game of compensation. Making my boss think it was their idea to pay me more. Finding an ally to convince my boss behind the scenes to pay me more. Having a client or a supplier send glowing notes about me right around performance review season. All with the goal to get me paid more.

And I even downplayed how I looked and appeared at work. I remember parking my BMW all the way in the back parking lot, not wanting anyone to know it was my car after I discovered my vice president and I drove the same year and model. I was a brand manager at the time.

"Why aren't you wearing your engagement ring to the leadership offsite?" my husband once asked me.

"I am up for a raise and a substantial bonus. I don't want to give them any reason not to give it to me."

"Yes," a girlfriend adamantly agreed with me when I confided to her how I was operating. "Sure, we own nice things, we have earned them. And we don't always need to wear them to work. Not the logo handbags, not the diamonds, and not those branded shoes. Don't give them another reason not to pay us what we know we have earned and deserve." And all this time, I thought I was alone in my mental exhaustion of calculating how I had to "show up" to earn my fair paycheck.

Over the course of my career, I also began to realize that this former manager said aloud what some leaders quietly think. And in my time coaching leaders, I have heard the following and more when it comes to why we even consider paying women less than what we might pay men. Here are rationalizations I have heard some leaders use in both private settings and in larger meetings:

"She's the primary earner in her family and won't ever leave. I wouldn't put her on the merit increase list."

"She is paid well enough."

"She's going out on maternity leave and who knows if she will come back. No need to give her a generous bonus this round."

"I know her husband who works in the sales division. He's killing it on commission, so we don't need to pay her any more."

"Did you see that Birkin bag she carries around? She doesn't need this job."

"She's single. She doesn't have a family. We should make it a priority to review the other team members' compensation first."

"She's not even asking for more money. So why are we reviewing her compensation?"

Now, pause and re-read the above statements. Except this time, substitute "she/her" with "he/his." Would we ever make these statements and assumptions, or ask these questions when it comes to discussing a man's compensation? When was the last time carrying a Birkin bag relevant to how much we paid him?

What is the Gender Pay Gap?

According to the Pew Research Center, the gender pay gap measures the difference in the median hourly earnings between men and women in the United States who work full- or part-time. The gender gap in pay hasn't changed much over the last 15 years.[1] According the U.S. Census Data, women earn 83 cents to every dollar earned by men.[2] This statistic however is misleading, an aggregated number that doesn't provide the complete picture.

It treats women as a monolith, not reflecting the truth, which is that women of color continue to suffer when it comes to compensation. Because the gender pay gap is much wider for the majority of women of color. Let's look at this study as an example:[3]

American Progress: Women of Color and the Gender Pay Gap

		White Men
Hispanic Women	$0.57	$1.00
Native American/Indigenous Women	$0.60	$1.00
Black Women	$0.64	$1.00
Asian American Pacific Islander Women (AAPI)	$0.85	$1.00

The Gender Pay Gap Statistic for AAPI Women Doesn't Reveal the True Economic Disparities

Even within a community, the gender pay gap doesn't tell the whole story. While the statistic shows that Asian American Pacific Islander (AAPI) women earn 85 cents to every dollar earned by men, the aggregate statistic hides the economic disparities among the AAPI subgroups. To start, the term AAPI includes more than 50 distinct ethnic groups.[4] And there are an estimated 12.7 million AAPI women in the United States.[5] This a diverse group of women, some of us working in higher wage roles in white collar jobs where we might have the option to work from home. And other AAPI women who are in lower wage roles, working in front-line jobs and in service sector roles.

(continued)

(*continued*)

One study showed that on average Indian women and Taiwanese women out-earn white men ($1.21 to $1.00), as well as Chinese women ($1.03 to $1.00), and Japanese women come close ($0.95 to $1.00).[6] However, Thai women earn $0.64, Vietnamese women earn $0.63, Cambodian women $0.60, and Burmese women earn $0.52 for every dollar a white man earns.[7] We cannot just simply generalize under the umbrella of AAPI without understanding the statistics making up each of these communities. Understanding these statistics (beyond just one study) is important to interrupting our biases on our journey to be more inclusive leaders, and ensuring we pay individuals fairly and equitably.

Economists, academics, and journalists have studied the gender pay gap for decades. While companies like Starbucks, Apple, Salesforce, Adobe, and Intel have been praised for the progress on wage equality for women,[8] overall progress to reach gender pay parity for women has been too slow across industries in the United States. As leaders, we think fixing the gender pay gap has very little to do with us. Because we say that it's the system that's broken. Or we may say the system isn't broken; we pay people based on "merit" and it has nothing to do with the fact they identify as a man or a woman. Some of us may have deep-seated biases when it comes to compensation—like my former manager. We may say, it's not our job, it's the job of Human Resources. Don't we already have enough to do? And finally, some of us may not admit that we are actually uncomfortable, weary, or anxious to talk about compensation. We may not even recognize the fact that we shut people down when it comes to the topic of compensation. Because we have our own unresolved issues when it comes to what money might mean to us: status, power, and wealth. We may have our own insecurities about how we equate our personal worth to our financial worth.

Growing up, I was raised not to to talk about money. And apparently, I am not alone. More than half of Americans avoid talking about money with friends.[9] So the chances are, we are less likely to talk about money at work. We would rather talk about politics and relationships with friends than discuss money.[10] Many of us grew up learning that it was rude to talk about money. My parents taught me to never ask someone how much they make or to discuss how much you make, or to ask how much something costs or was worth. We also never spoke about "money" in the less obvious ways: where we lived, where we went on vacation, where we went to school, what kind of cars we drove, how we celebrated big family occasions. It wasn't until well into my adulthood years that I discovered how much my father made working as an executive and what my mother made in her teaching career.

It took me years to break the silence and learn how to talk about money. For so long, I was discouraged from being loud about money and encouraged to stay silent. And the more I started to read about money, to talk about money, to think about money, over time it slowly became easier to talk about my own compensation. I compared notes with friends in similar industries, got negotiating tips from my husband, and asked mentors for advice on my compensation packages throughout my career. I took notes from Alexandra Carter's book *Ask for More*. Yet just when so many of us walked into work again with the confidence to ask for more, we were told to stay silent. Like my former manager, some leaders continue to use silence as a tool of oppression. So how can we close the gender pay gap if we aren't allowed to ask about our compensation?

Let's Talk About Money

As leaders, we need to take personal accountability for ensuring our teams are paid fairly and equitably. And that starts with understanding our own feelings about money. Let's self-reflect on the following questions to help understand and unlock what stops us from being open to talking about compensation:

- Are you personally anxious or uncomfortable when it comes to the topic of money? If you have anxiety about this topic, from where do you think that stems?
- What do you recall about your childhood and your relationship with money? Do you have any memories (positive or negative) associated with money?
- Do you talk to family and friends about money (e.g., tips on investing, advice for salary negotiations, questions about buying a home) or is this a topic you shy away from? Why?
- How do you define your personal worth versus how you define your financial worth?
- If someone on your team approaches you to have their compensation reviewed, how does that make you feel? Do you feel yourself shutting down or do you approach the conversation with an open mind? Does your reaction change if it's a man versus a woman?
- Are you happy they approached you about their compensation and are advocating for themselves? Or do you find yourself thinking they are ungrateful and unappreciative of what the organization has done for them? Does your reaction change if it's a man versus a woman?
- What would happen if everyone on your team knew how each team member was compensated? Would that cause you anxiety or give you a sense of relief? Why?

We as leaders have a responsibility in breaking the silence when it comes to compensation at work. Individuals feel included when they feel seen, when they belong, and when they are valued. Value isn't about free fancy gluten-free snacks, meditation apps, nap pods, Ping-Pong tables, and an endless supply of ice cream. "Show me the money," once was famously said by the characters in the movie *Jerry McGuire*. Because I don't need another free black hoodie or my salted peanut butter with chocolate flecks scoops of ice cream. I need to be paid for my expertise and for my accomplishments. I need to be paid what I am worth.

Let's ask ourselves the ways in which we can take personal accountability for helping to close the gender pay gap. And also ask ourselves how we can influence what processes our organization chooses to implement to ensure we are paying everyone fairly and equitably. Here's a starting point:

1. Communicate Your Pay Equity Measures

Your company should undergo a pay equity analysis,[11] and if you haven't, now is the time to influence and stress the importance of it as a leader. Once complete, communicate to your organization the overall findings. This shows you are focused on ensuring all employees are being valued fairly for their contributions. The pressure on companies is intensifying to increase transparency around the gender pay gap. From mandates reporting requirements and state laws, to shareholder activism, companies need to get ahead of understanding what gaps they need to close and help lead setting industry best practices. Don't wait for a lawsuit to be the reason you address pay with your organization.

Six months after I asked that former manager to review my compensation, I saw in my Workday profile that I had been given a 5 percent pay increase. There was no communication on why this happened. The increase just appeared and then reflected in my pay-check. It was a small step closer to being paid what my compensation should have been.

As a leader, be clear on when raises happen and how they are determined. Are they based on the market fluctuations? Are they based on performance? Do you do off-cycle adjustments, and how are those handled to minimize bias? If you are adjusting an employee's pay, let them know the rationale behind it. Especially if you discovered systemic bias and are taking corrective action.

If individuals do have questions about their compensation, they shouldn't be limited to only asking their bosses. Ensure that Human Resources Business Partners and the Compensation team are open to being approached regarding questions on compensation. They should be armed with the data to understand all the factors that reflect the individual's compensation within the organization.

2. Challenge Leaders on Who They Reward

Her spouse makes more than enough money. She is the sole breadwinner in her family. Her partner lost her job so she needs this job. Some leaders will rely on these biases and more to justify why they decide to pay a woman less. And pay a man on the team more.

We know our biases surface under stress and when we multi-task.[12] During a global crisis like the COVID-19 pandemic and during other moments of economic downturns, leaders were under enormous pressure to make decisions on furloughs, pay cuts, and lay-offs. We need to interrupt our biases and ask: if this were a man, would we use these same justifications and rationale to pay him less?

And in those moments when we are working hard to to retain talent, we may turn to spot bonuses or retention bonuses to get talent to stay. It can help retain top performers and help them feel valued and seen. HR Business Partners must oversee this with leaders, to

interrupt bias and ensure men don't receive these bonuses dispropor-
tionately more than women.

Finally, many of us have been conditioned to equate compensation to only the base salary. The Carta Equity Summit Report showed
that for every dollar in equity that men collectively own, women own
just 47 cents.[13] Equity is one of the biggest drivers of wealth creation
in Silicon Valley and beyond. Ensure as a leader you are frequently
monitoring who receives equity grants, how much, and why.

3. Consider a No-Negotiating Salary Policy

Reddit, Magoosh, and Elevations Credit Union are just a few of the
companies that have a no-negotiating salary policy for candidates.[14] This helps close the gender pay gap and level the playing field.
If a candidate is uncomfortable negotiating, they might not ask for
more money and accept the offer, which puts them at a disadvantage
versus other candidates who negotiate and are successful in getting
more money. If the recruiting or hiring manager is uncomfortable
with the fact that a particular candidate is asking for more, as in the
case of my former boss, they may shut down the negotiations even if
there may be room in the budget to pay the candidate more. Setting
a culture of "no negotiations allowed" can ensure that you pay consistent and fair salaries.

To structure your policy for success, determine first what a fair
and equitable compensation target means for the roles and levels for
which you are recruiting. Ensure you are competitive within the
industry and the geography, utilizing third-party consultants and data
to validate.[15]

Next, ensure you let all candidates know at the start of the recruiting process about your no-negotiating salary policy. Candidates can
then opt-out of the process at the start. This will prevent any surprises
at the end of the process when they realize they can't negotiate.

Finally, there can be no exception to your policy. Candidates might not believe the policy, and still try to negotiate.[16] Recruiters and leaders have to adhere to the policy to ensure individuals are paid on merit and not on their ability or inability to negotiate. And remember, negotiations may not be well received by the recruiter, depending on who is asking for more money and the recruiter's biases.

4. Ensure Mothers Aren't Penalized

According to the National Women's Law Center, mothers working full time, year-round, are paid 70 cents for every dollar paid to working fathers. This gap means $1,500 a month, or $18,000 per year, in lost income for mothers working outside the home.[17] This gap in pay is known as the motherhood penalty and is worse for moms of color.[18] The motherhood penalty is still alive despite the fact that mothers are more qualified than ever. According to the Pew Research Center, 80 percent of women with a PhD or professional degree gave birth in 2014, versus 65 percent in 1994.[19] And during the pandemic, mothers continued to be a large percentage of essential and frontline workers. Yet they continue to be paid less than their male counterparts. The wage gap for mothers has only closed by 4 cents since 2007.[20]

Fathers, on the other hand, benefit from the fatherhood premium or fatherhood bonus. Men often receive a salary increase when they become fathers,[21] where average earnings can increase by than 6 percent.[22] Another study, reaffirming the fatherhood premium, showed that fathers make roughly 20 percent more than men with no children.[23]

"When men have children, they are seen as responsible and stable—'He has a family to support,'" said Sallie Krawcheck, co-founder and CEO of Ellevest, a former Wall Street executive, and mother of two.[24] There may be a number of factors at play as to why mothers are paid less than fathers, including leaving the workforce for an extended period and working a reduced schedule. And some leaders may continue to discriminate against mothers, assuming they aren't as committed, distracted by other priorities, and aren't interested or invested in growing their career long-term.

Pay equity analysis should pay special attention to the moments when women began to expand their families. Ensure new mothers are not penalized financially for taking parental leave (we'll discuss parental leave more in a bit). Continue to watch for compensation discrepancies as both women and men expand their families. Monitor promotion as well as attrition rates; working mothers should be given access to the same opportunities for advancement as working fathers.

Finally, for many caregivers, including mothers, the pandemic changed the way we work. Many employers now offer increased flexibility for all their employees. For many mothers and caregivers, being able to work remotely or have more flexible schedules gives them the freedom to work while also caring for their families. Make sure to watch for the rise of remote location or proximity bias, which can be a preference for those who are in the office or come into the office more, with close physical proximity to leaders (we will discuss this bias in more detail later). Ensure that the increased flexibility for mothers, and caregivers, doesn't mean they are penalized by being paid less versus those employees who go into the office.

5. Address Women's Concerns Before They Resign

According to a Randstad U.S. study, 60 percent of women say they have never negotiated with their current organizations regarding their pay.[25] This could also be a driver as to why women are much more likely than men to leave, making the lateral move to another organization to increase their salary. Women would rather pursue external opportunities than to stay and negotiate internally for what they deserve. They might fear appearing too demanding, being unlikeable, and concerned how their manager and organization will react to their request.

Don't enable a culture where you minimize, dismiss, guilt trip, or gaslight a woman for asking to have her compensation reviewed. My former manager continued to gaslight me following my attempt to have him review my compensation. A few weeks after our conversation, my boss took my team and me out to lunch. Shortly after we placed our lunch orders, he loudly announced: "Mita has done great work, but I have paid her more than fairly over the years." He knew I had been undervalued for my contributions. His own biases about me prevented his paying me equitably. I eventually left that organization and his team.

Women shouldn't have to ask to have their compensation reviewed. As leaders, it's our job to ensure they feel valued, recognized, and are paid equitably for their work. If we can't fulfill this promise to them, let's not be surprised when they decide to resign and leave to go work for an organization that will.

6. Finally, Don't Be So Quick to "Celebrate" Equal Pay Day

Before you and your company post, tweet, share, and talk about the importance of Equal Pay Day, ask yourself the following question: what are you personally doing to close the gender pay gap? According to the National Committee on Pay Equity, the date signifies "how far into the year women must work to earn what men earned in the previous year."[26] As we have seen, the gender pay gap varies significantly for women of color. Additional Equal Pay Days have been added to reflect this disparity, including Asian American, Native Hawaiian and Pacific Islander Women's Equal Pay Day, Mom's Equal Pay Day, Native Women's Equal Pay Day, Latina's Equal Pay Day, and Black Women's Equal Pay Day.[27]

I remember a leader once approaching me on Black Women's Equal Pay Day. He asked, "Can you help me post a note of celebration for Black Women's Equal Pay Day?" I had to coach him that this wasn't a celebration: it reflected how much further into the year Black women had to work to make what white men made (in this year, the date fell in late September). I also told him the most important thing he could do to honor the moment was to make sure all the Black women who worked for him, and the ones who worked with him, were being paid fairly and equitably. He was quiet for a minute and admitted he had never thought of that before.

So, when it comes to pay, women don't need fixing. We don't always need to take another negotiations course. We don't always need to find our voice. We don't always need to work on our confidence. Many are ready to discuss, advocate, and fight for our rightful compensation. We need the leaders in charge of writing our paychecks to be willing to have these conversations and to start valuing us for who we are and what we do. For what we consistently bring to the organization and the impact we continue to make. Remember, inclusion is about having a seat at the table and ensuring that your voice is heard and matters. And inclusion is also about being valued:

It's about ensuring you are being paid for what you have earned and what you deserve.

Tips on How You Can Help Close the Gender Pay Gap at Work

- **Don't wait for Human Resources to fix pay inequities.**
  It's your responsibility to know if each member of your team is being paid fairly and equitably. Don't wait for someone else to do your job. Partner with Human Resources and your team to understand where pay inequities exist. Fight to close those pay gaps.

(continued)

- **Remember that compensation is more than just base salary.**

  Beyond analyzing the base salary, remember to look at annual bonuses, equity and stock grants, one-time bonuses or awards, travel stipends, and other rewards. Get a holistic picture of how you may be valuing individuals differently.

- **Proactively address compensation with your team.**

  During performance reviews, actively address compensation with your team. Don't wait for them to bring it up. Let them know they are being paid fairly and equitably and that you have done your research. And if they should be getting paid more, let them know you are fighting to fix any gaps.

- **Advocate for others who aren't being paid equitably.**

  Use your power and influence to help those outside of your team. I once had a white team leader (not my boss but one who had a seat on the Executive team) fight for my pay behind the scenes. It made all the difference in helping increase my compensation. And check out Alexandra Carter's book *Ask for More* to have a negotiation coach in your corner.

- **Interrupt bias when it comes to conversations about pay.**

  Why does it matter if Mita is the primary breadwinner in her family? Would we be asking these questions if Mita was a man? How is this a factor in how much we pay her? Interrupt bias when you see it in action when it comes to pay. Ask open-ended questions and challenge individuals to interrupt their bias. Ensure you focus the discussion on making sure individuals are being valued for their expertise and their accomplishments.

7 We Need More People of Color in Leadership. Let's Launch a Mentorship Program!

After reviewing the most recent workforce metrics at a quarterly talent review meeting, a senior leader exclaimed, "We need more people of color in leadership. Let's launch a mentorship program!" She was excited about her lightbulb moment, trying to corral those in the room to back her idea. In the meeting, there was one leader of color, and me. He avoided eye contact with me as he continued to peck away at his keyboard.

"How do we think a mentorship program will help more people of color become directors and above here?" I asked, hoping to introduce another solution.

"Because we will mentor them, of course. We will share with them how we got to where we are in our careers," she explained.

"Seems like a solid approach," someone else chimed in, as he kept scrolling on his phone, waiting for the meeting to end.

"Who are we going to include in this program?" someone else asked.

"Oh, Black and Hispanic talent," another leader bellowed from across the table. "Let's focus on those groups only." Everyone else nodded and agreed as the meeting abruptly ended.

As he walked out, that leader approached me and said, "We have enough Asians here, probably even too many given how big we are. Just focus on Black and Hispanic."

During the course of my career, I have observed that mentorship programs can often be the catch-all, go-to, and must implement solution to any talent issue your organization faces. Is your talent leaving because they don't have enough leadership and development opportunities? Launch a mentorship program. Are you unable to give raises this year but need to recognize your talent? Launch a mentorship program. Are you unclear what your Employee Resource Groups should be doing? Ask them to launch a mentorship program. Are you puzzled why more people of color aren't in leadership positions in your organization? Well, it's time to launch a mentorship program. It's the key to being "more inclusive."

Among the Fortune 500 companies, approximately 70 percent of them have mentorship programs.[1]

According to research published in the *Harvard Business Review*, individuals who have strong mentors see the long-lasting impact on their careers: they advance more rapidly, they earn more money, and they also just enjoy their careers more.[2] And yet so many mentorship programs fail, fall flat, and just fizzle out.

I have lost count of all the mentorship programs I raised my hand for and all the ones I was forced into in my career. All with the singular promise of developing me and helping me advance my career. There was the time I was matched with someone who was at the same level, was very nice, and had little to no career advice for me. We bonded over our obsession with *Keeping up with the Kardashians*. There was the time I was matched with a very senior leader. We had a great first two meetings. On the third meeting, I waited for 30 minutes for him to show up. The next day, while in casual conversation with another colleague, they told me "my mentor" had been transferred to London. But the mentor never shared that small detail with me. There was another mentor who incessantly talked about herself and ended up asking me for lots of advice. I became the unofficial mentor in that relationship, including helping her with her social media (they now call this reverse-mentoring). And another mentoring pairing, where he showed up once, and I thought we had a good discussion. He never responded to any of my emails or attempts to schedule a follow-up. He completely ghosted me. Even when weeks later I saw him in the cafeteria and waved, he didn't wave back. It was as if he had no idea who I was.

Too often, launching mentorship programs becomes a check the box exercise for leaders so we can move on to the next task. Because the truth is, even when mentorship programs are executed successfully, as research indicates, let's ask ourselves, who do we think benefits from mentorship?

Because if this idea of mentoring and companywide mentorship programs benefited everyone equally, wouldn't we see more people of color in leadership positions across our organizations? We must stop believing the myth that mentorship programs are enough to get people of color into leadership roles and build more inclusive organizations.

Who Do You Choose to Mentor and Why?

Over the course of our careers, many of us will find ourselves in mentoring relationships. We will find ourselves helping and supporting others in their careers. Take a look at the following questions and self-reflect on your answers:

- What does mentoring someone at work mean to you?
- Is mentoring something you look forward to? Or do you find it too distracting, and a drain on your energy and time at work? Does it depend on who you are mentoring?
- What drives your decision to want to mentor someone in your organization?
- How do you show up as a mentor? How do you showcase your commitment to your mentee?
- When you mentor someone, do you check-in with their boss on what their career goals are and how they are progressing? Do you understand why they may be stalling in their career?
- If you think about all the people you have mentored, what are some of the characteristics they have in common with you and with each other?
- Do you have a pattern of mentoring individuals who look like you, act like you, and think like you? If yes, why do you think that is?
- Have you ever considered the importance of diversity of representation when thinking about who you choose to mentor and give your time to?

Here's the truth about my own career: I don't need another mentor. Because throughout my career, I have been over-mentioned and under-sponsored. I came to this realization when my career sponsor, Gail Tifford, once shared the most game-changing piece of career advice I had ever received: "Do you know who is talking about you and your career when the doors are closed?"

Mentorship is different from sponsorship. We may assign a mentor when new hires join our team, when individuals move divisions within a company or move abroad for an international assignment. Someone who can help us find the bathrooms and cafeteria, who can teach us how to use key systems. Someone who can help us understand our manager's leadership style, the importance of delivering one project over another, and recommend the best agency to help make a cost-effective video with a 48-hour turnaround.

Mentors are important for professional and personal development. I have many mentors whom I call for advice on the best way to present a controversial recommendation; for advice on how to deliver tough feedback to my team; the best restaurant in midtown New York City for a client meeting; for an introduction to a nonprofit I would like to volunteer with. And here's the important distinction: my mentors aren't always working in my organization or in a position of power to directly help me advance my career.

I have had the privilege of mentoring many people of color throughout their career. Here's one of the first things I now ask them: Who is advocating for your career when you aren't in the room? If they aren't able to answer that question or, like me, they had never even considered the question, herein lies one of the critical barriers to their career advancement.

Here's how a sponsor is different than a mentor. In my experience, sponsors have typically been two levels above me. They have worked in my organization; they know who the key power players are and the politics of how things work. They have a sizeable budget and oversee a significant part of the business. They have the power to pay and promote individuals. They are sitting behind those closed doors when talent decisions are made, influencing who is up for which next assignment. Finally, they see the value in what I bring to the table and the impact I make in the organization. They use their own political capital to get me a meeting with the CEO; to have me present at a companywide meeting; to nominate me to represent the company externally for a strategic partnership; to get my name on the list for a key role that hasn't even been posted; to ensure I am considered for a merit increase. They are actively sponsoring my career.

When I work with leaders who say they are firmly invested in building a workforce that represents the changing demographics of our country, I ask: "Who are you fighting for behind closed doors? Whose career are you invested in advancing?" In many cases, they are drawn to sponsoring the careers of individuals who look like them, act like them, and think like them. And imagine the ripple effect that can have across your organization over time. And then you find yourself sitting in a meeting with peers, reviewing workforce metrics, where most everyone is baffled as to why there aren't more people of color in leadership roles in your organization.

This is where a sponsorship program focused on the advancement of people of color in your organization can be a game-changer.

Asian Colleagues Don't Need Our Help: Debunking the "Model Minority" Myth

"You people are all successful," another leader once said to me. "Getting promoted faster than white men and making more money than all of us. We don't need to be focused on how we can help our Asian colleagues here. They have more than enough help."

To this day, those comments made behind closed doors still haunt me. Because he was bold enough to say aloud what too many individuals silently agree with—comments embodying the very essence of the "model minority" myth. Here are three ways in which leaders can debunk the model minority myth in our workplaces:

First, educate yourself on what the "model minority" myth is

Sociologist William Petersen coined the "model minority"[3] myth. In the 1960s, he wrote in *New York Magazine* about how many Japanese American families, despite everything the government put them through (including during World War II being forced into internment and pushed to enlist in their military to prove their allegiance), rose above it all. They were hardworking, well educated, even well dressed, and succeeding despite all odds with help from no one. They were the model minority.

Over the decades, this myth has persisted. It is an incredibly dangerous and damaging stereotype that paints Asian Americans and Pacific Islanders (AAPI) all as being incredibly successful, high-achieving, and hardworking overachievers. This also paints the picture that the AAPI community is more successful than any other group or community and free of problems, obstacles, or challenges. When we position the AAPI community as the "model minority," we assume, just as that leader did, they don't need any help. We erase and don't accept the ways in which our AAPI colleagues are discriminated against in our workplaces, including facing daily microaggressions, being passed up for promotion opportunities, and not always being paid fairly and equitably.

Second, understand why it's a myth

Let's start by understanding that the model minority myth is in fact a myth. It's a widely held false belief that anyone who identifies as AAPI doesn't need help or assistance and is incredibly

(continued)

(continued)

high achieving and wildly successful. The model minority myth is a dangerous and harmful stereotype, which helps reinforce other false beliefs including:

- All AAPI individuals are/were straight-A students.
- All AAPI individuals are good at math and science.
- All AAPI individuals come from wealthy, two-parent, stable households.

It's important to understand the AAPI community encompasses a diverse diaspora, including approximately 50 ethnic groups speaking over 100 languages—a group with ties to Chinese, Indian, Japanese, Filipino, Vietnamese, Korean, Hawaiian, and other AAPI ancestries.[4]

According to a *New York Times* study, despite having the highest median income of any community, the AAPI community also has the largest income gap. For example, in New York City, AAPI individuals experience the highest poverty rates versus any other immigrant group.[5]

When we perpetuate the myth that AAPI individuals don't need support, we render the community invisible. It reframes their experience as a community who are not people of color and dismisses the fact that they face racism.

Third, interrupt bias on your teams when it comes to the myth

Once we understand this myth, we can interrupt bias when we see it occur on our teams and in our workplaces. As we also continue to invest in building relationships with AAPI colleagues, we will be better equipped to interrupt the bias. We can educate others on the opportunity to also include AAPI colleagues in our DEI plans along with other communities. It's an opportunity to include, and not exclude, further rendering the AAPI community invisible.

Let's start with looking at data points that provide a small snapshot of our workplaces. The Black community is approximately 12.4 percent of the U.S. population.[6] Yet they only account for 8 percent of those in professional roles. Black professionals make up only 3.2 percent of all senior leadership roles, and less than 1 percent of all Fortune 500 CEO positions.[7] The Hispanic community represents approximately 18.7 percent of the U.S. population. Research shows that Hispanic individuals only make up approximately 4 percent of senior leadership roles at large U.S. companies.[8] According to the Brooking Institute, by 2045, white individuals will make up 49.7 percent of the population, versus 24.6 percent for Hispanic individuals, 13.1 percent for Black individuals, 7.9 percent for AAPI individuals, and 3.8 percent for multiracial individuals.[9] It is clear that people of color will continue to be key to driving our nation's growth, and they must have a seat at leadership tables across our companies.

The need to include Black and Hispanic talent in initiatives like a sponsorship program is clear. What about AAPI talent? This is where the myth comes in. When looking at the AAPI community, they represent approximately 6 percent of the U.S. population.[10] While the AAPI community represents 12 percent of the U.S. professional workforce, their careers stall. AAPI leaders are absent from the C-suite. Less than 1 percent of S&P 500 CEOs are of East Asian descent.[11] Contrary to what the myth would tell us, AAPI colleagues are the least likely group to be promoted into management roles, when compared

(continued)

with Black and Hispanic talent. They are often left out of the "glass ceiling" conversation.[12]

This is where sponsors can play a significant role in ensuring that AAPI colleagues are included in your company's DEI plans, because they too face microaggressions and discrimination in our workplaces. Because for decades, this model minority myth has kept AAPI colleagues out of conversations on equity, holding our colleagues back. At work, the myth can often pigeonhole AAPI colleagues into only technical roles. They can be seen as less vocal, timid, and deferential and not given the opportunity to showcase their ability to lead teams. Sponsors can help by advocating for AAPI colleagues to take on skill-stretching projects, where they can build and demonstrate their leadership skills and strategic capabilities. Sponsors can help ensure they are not overlooked for promotion opportunities along with being compensated fairly and equitably for their contributions.

What Makes a Sponsorship Program Work

Setting up a sponsorship program takes time and commitment. Before rushing to start a sponsorship program, be thoughtful about how you can start this initiative in your organization.

Consider and reflect on the following four questions as you embark on this journey:

What Does a Sponsorship Pairing Look Like?

A sponsorship pairing consists of two individuals: a sponsor and a rising star. They both need to be working in the same organization for a sponsorship program to be effective. In my experience of building sponsorship programs, the sponsor needs to be typically at least two levels higher than the rising star. The sponsor will be someone who has significant experience, influence, and is respected and listened to by their peers. In many organizations, it is likely a sponsor will be white, and often a man. This will particularly hold true in fields where white women and women of color are underrepresented, including fields based in science, technology, and engineering.[13]

The rising star will be someone identified as having the potential to join a leadership team or sit in the C-Suite someday. They need the right support, access, and development opportunities to help them advance their careers. The rising star should work on an initiative or sit in a part of an organization the sponsor is naturally invested in.

When looking at creating a sponsorship program for people of color, consider rising stars who identify with communities where you lack the most representation at senior levels.

Once when working with leaders on this exercise, they said, "We need more Black talent in the C-Suite. But we have no one in the pipeline. We have no Black talent who are rising stars in our organization."

I asked in response: "In your organization, how do you define who a rising star is? What's the track record of success and metrics you are looking at? Have you considered there may be rising stars who are under the radar, talent who you just don't know about yet?"

What's the Role of the Sponsor?

A sponsor uses their political and social capital to advance the rising star's career. Over time, a sponsor will be more than a sounding board for seeking advice on topics like "what your next career move should be" or "advice on how to ask for stock-based compensation" or "who else you should know in this organization." A sponsor will get your name on a slate for a job you didn't even know was available. A sponsor will advocate for you to get a bigger bonus, or even a retention bonus, as management works in a competitive market to keep strong talent. A sponsor will appoint you for a special taskforce that gets you direct exposure to the CEO. All of this occurs with the sponsor and the sponsor's peers, behind those "closed doors" when they are talking about you and your career. Finally, the sponsor has a responsibility to nurture this relationship with the rising star. The sponsor must make the commitment to connect consistently and be present and available for this individual. For the sponsor, this will also likely be the start of an important cross-cultural work relationship.

The Sponsor Effect

Many of my views on career sponsorship have been informed by the work of Sylvia Ann Hewlett. Kennedy Ihezie introduced me to Sylvia, who is a thought leader and economist. After meeting with Sylvia, she asked if I would be interviewed in her book *The Sponsor Effect*.

In the book, I discuss how my sponsor, Jonathan Atwood, was instrumental to my career success. He put my name up for a job I didn't know was available. He personally advocated for me to meet with the CEO to interview for that job. Jonathan put my name up for speaking opportunities, like the Bentonville Film Festival sponsored by Walmart, where I was on a panel with actress and activist Geena Davis. As a member of the U.S. leadership team, he helped me get opportunities to present to that group. He gave me specific feedback on how to strengthen recommendations and gave me a political read of the room (e.g., the CEO will have these two concerns, the head of supply chain will likely ask you this question). We are still in touch to this day, where he continues to connect me with leaders and recommend me for advisory roles.

Finally, in *The Sponsor Effect*, Sylvia makes the case for why leaders need to be sponsors. And that investing in others makes you a better leader. Senior executives who sponsor rising talent are 53 percent more likely to be promoted than those who don't. Sylvia says when leaders choose to sponsor, those individuals contribute "stellar performance, steadfast loyalty, and capabilities that you, the sponsors, may lack, increasing how fast and far you can go."[14] This is a must-read for any leader on their journey to be a more inclusive leader who wants an in-depth understanding of how powerful sponsorship can be.

What Is the Role of The Rising Star?

The rising star equally must make the commitment to connect consistently and be present and available for this relationship with their sponsor. And why would a sponsor use their political and social capital to advance someone else's career? It's because the rising star is someone who consistently over-delivers, making significant impact to the organization. The sponsor has visibility to their work and is personally invested in what the rising star is working on. The #1 job of the rising star is to continue performing, making impact, and being a valuable asset to the organization so the sponsor fulfills their #1 job: to help advance the rising star's career.

As the rising star, there are many moments where you will have to be brave. To go out of your comfort zone. To develop a relationship with someone who in most cases will not look like you, who will have different life experiences than you, and who you might believe you have nothing in common with. And you will also have to fight through your own biases on what you think someone is like on the surface, to make the concerted effort to get to know them as an individual. Remember, you won't be alone in this; your sponsor will also be there as a partner in this relationship.

How Do You Select Sponsorship Pairings?

Once you have reviewed your workforce demographics, agree to the level of the sponsor and the rising star. For example, if you are focused on increasing representation of Black talent at the director level, select

Black talent who are at a manager or senior manager level, and select sponsors who are at a vice president level. Titles and levels will vary from company to company, and the key is to ensure a sponsor, who in this example is a vice president, is someone at the right level who has the power and influence to promote directors.

Create a list of potential sponsors within the senior leadership team. After creating a list of sponsors, meet with each of them one-on-one to ensure they understand, are aligned with, and believe in the objective of the sponsorship program: to advance more people of color into leadership in your organization. It is critical that sponsors understand the objective and the role they play in this relationship before they are invited to officially participate and are introduced to the rising star. Once you kick off the program for the pairs with an official invite, make clear it's the sponsor's responsibility to set up the first "get to know you" meeting between the pair.

The selection of rising stars should involve the senior leadership team and the sponsors (there may be some overlap between these two groups, which is expected, e.g., the Chief Marketing Officer is on the senior leadership team and also becomes a sponsor). Even as we use the words "rising star," check for unconscious bias on who gets selected and why. Everyone must work from the same definition of what a "rising star" means in your function and in your organization. Clarity on the criteria of how you identify who is selected ties back to their performance and delivery of results for the organization.

Finally, these pairings need to be mutually beneficial. This isn't about mentorship—this is about sponsorship. The sponsor must feel invested in the rising star's work to help advance their career. For example, you may choose to pair the vice president of supply chain with a manager in finance because this manager is working on a companywide cost savings initiative that would include inputs from supply chain. Or you choose to pair a senior marketing manager with the Chief Financial Officer because this manager is reviewing all the media investments in their division over the last year and analyzing the return on investment. Understand what the rising star is working on and who else in the organization would be invested in the outcome of that work to make the best sponsor match.

Sponsorship can be the game-changer. Imagine if every senior leader who fit the criteria of what it takes to be a sponsor decided to act. They decided to sponsor the career of just one colleague of color to personally help them develop and advance their careers. Imagine the ripple effect it could have across our organizations and how different the idea of inclusion would look and feel. So ask yourself the following question: Whose career, other than your own, are you willing to advocate and fight for starting tomorrow?

Tips for Building a Sponsorship Program Focusing on Advancing People of Color

1. **Consider pairing a rising star with a sponsor who is not their manager, or their manager's manager.** It gives the rising star access to a network outside of their immediate team. A boss should already be an advocate for their team member's career. And if the boss is not an advocate, it provides an opportunity for the rising star to build a meaningful relationship with another senior leader who can be a sponsor.

2. **Pilot a sponsorship program as a first step if this concept is newer to your organization.** Start with 12 sponsorship pairs for a larger organization, 2 to 6 pairs for small to medium-sized organizations. Choose a function or a division where you can ensure you have the buy-in and support of senior leadership. Have the senior leader host a

(continued)

kick-off to discuss the importance of the program with all the pairs. As a follow-up to the kick-off, host sessions separately for the group of sponsors and group of rising stars to review their roles and responsibilities. Be clear on commitments, including the pair meeting at least six times a year and the sponsor being involved in career planning for the rising star. Once the pilot is up and running, scale the program across the organization. Measure progress over 12 months and 24 months to see the impact the relationship has had on the rising star's career. This is where having a DEI team becomes critical so they can help drive the pilot program and set it up for success.

3. **Ask sponsor and rising star pairs to attend events together as a way to further develop their relationship.** This can include DEI events or Employee Resource Group led events. It can also be attending your company's monthly town hall, where afterward the pair can discuss the state of the business together. In today's virtual world, the sponsor and rising star can also attend a variety of virtual programming from the comfort of their own homes, and then discuss afterward their thoughts over a virtual coffee connect.

4. **Embed the sponsorship program in your performance evaluation process.** For the rising star's performance review, ensure the sponsor is involved in the evaluation process along with their manager. And we should be asking all senior leaders during their performance evaluations: Who are you sponsoring? How are you helping them develop and advance in their career?

5. **Check-in on these relationships to see how they are progressing.** Check-in with both the sponsor and the rising star individually, in one-on-one meetings and through group surveys. This is another important way to build cross-cultural relationships at work, and it's up to both individuals to invest the time and effort to grow and nurture this relationship. These relationships should continue long after the formal sponsorship ends, or as individuals inevitably move on to other companies. If the relationship isn't developing, diagnose what the issue might be. Is it a lack of commitment or time? Is the sponsor disengaged and, if so, why? Address the issues head on before formally dissolving the pairing and introducing the rising star to another sponsor.

8

Of Course We Support Women! We Just Extended Maternity Leave.

"Of course we support women! We just extended maternity leave," the leader scoffed, throwing his hands in the air. "So how can we be losing women faster than we are hiring them?"

The leaders had seemed perplexed by the attrition data. The rumors in the organization had been swirling for weeks: women were resigning and moving on to other opportunities because they didn't feel supported. And this set of leaders had been the ones to sign off on the additional funding to extend maternity leave to 20 weeks.

"Oh, well, we know women are quitting to stay home and watch their kids," said another leader, adamantly. "They are also leaving to follow their husbands' careers. In fact, I know two women on my team whose husbands got jobs on the West Coast. And, well, I couldn't have them work remotely, that just didn't make sense. So of course they had to resign."

"From what I am seeing from the exit interview data is that women aren't resigning to stay home," I said, jumping into the conversation. "The majority of the women who resigned say they didn't feel supported after they came back from leave, after they became mothers. They are leaving for promotions they aren't getting here, heading to smaller to mid-sized companies where they can get more equity as part of their compensation . . ."

"Listen, if women are choosing to stay home so be it," another leader interrupted me, ignoring my insights from the exit interview data. "They just can't blame us for that."

One of the biggest myths I see leaders believing is that by extending maternity leave, and checking the box with other policies, that alone will help attract, develop, and promote women. Focusing only on maternity leave isn't the catch-all solution to supporting new mothers. Focusing only on maternity leave doesn't help mothers ensure they aren't mommy tracked, and that their careers aren't slowed down. Finally, focusing only on maternity leave perpetuates the idea that all women are mothers or want to become mothers. Because when we continue to focus on the one thing we have done (yes, we have great maternity leave, let's pat ourselves on the back), we use that as a distraction and choose to ignore all the other ways we aren't showing up as inclusive leaders for women.

Focus on Parental Leave, Not Maternity Leave

More and more companies are offering parental leave, versus maternity leave. Parental leave offers time off after the adoption or birth of a child regardless of parent gender, for all new parents. When we use the language of maternity leave, it can leave out employees who don't identify as women; nor does it include foster care, adoption, or surrogacy. And for birthing mothers, companies also offer paid pregnancy-related leave (as part of their short-term disability insurance). Focusing on and implementing parental leave is more inclusive, which enables mothers and fathers to equally bond with their children and to share parenting responsibilities more equitably. We will cover the importance of parental leave more in the next chapter.

When we think of how we can support women, we need to ensure they are not just surviving but thriving in our organizations. We need to start by looking at our systems and processes that are failing women. And we need to think about how we are showing up in the moments that matter in a woman's career. Let's start by asking ourselves three questions to consider how our organizations can better support and advance women's careers in our journey to build more inclusive cultures:

1. Have You Created a Broader Ecosystem to Support New Mothers?

A few weeks into my first maternity leave, a former colleague and friend called to check on me and my infant son, Jay. (My employer at the time didn't offer parental leave.) It had been a rough birth physically and happened in Manhattan, in the aftermath of Hurricane Sandy, which added to the stress. I welcomed her call, thankful to hear her familiar voice.

"How are you doing?" she asked me gently, as we swapped new mom stories and made plans to meet up soon. "Is everything okay job-wise? Are you still planning to return to work?"

"Oh yes," I replied quickly, changing my son's diaper as we spoke. "Why wouldn't I?"

She was silent for a moment, then said, "A recruiter called me about your job, and it's also posted online, so I thought you weren't coming back. I'm sorry to be the one to have to tell you."

I don't remember what I said next. I don't remember how the call ended. I do remember that my head was spinning. I finished feeding my son and put him down for a nap.

Why would my job be posted online when I was going back? Why were they looking to backfill me when I was on maternity leave? Why hadn't anyone told me?

I thought back to the period before I'd taken leave. When the doctor advised me to stop traveling to customer meetings in my third trimester, my bosses weren't happy. When I stayed at the office until 11 p.m. to work on urgent requests at seven months pregnant, no one ever suggested that I order dinner. (I recall finding old airline crackers in my bag.) When I wrapped up things a few days before my due date, management assured me that I would come back to my role. But now I didn't trust them. I resigned toward the end of my maternity leave after finding another opportunity.

The lesson I drew from this was simple. Maternity leave is one thing. Support for new mothers is an entirely different issue.

Asha Santos, an employment attorney who advises U.S. companies on employment law and how to build respect in the workplace, agrees: "How a woman is treated in the months leading up to her maternity leave and then during leave and shortly thereafter when she returns to work will determine whether or not a company will be able to retain her," she explains.[1]

According to the Society for Human Resource Management (SHRM), 55 percent of organizations offer paid maternity leave and 45 percent offer paid paternity leave.[2] And many organizations have increased the length of maternity leave and parental leave as well.[3] Some organizations are also making policies more inclusive:

Spotify, Etsy, Twitter, and more offer paid parental leave for both birth and non-birth parents to step in and fill the void in countries like the United States where no mandated paid parental leave exists.[4,5,6]

But paid time off is not enough. Consider the following as your organization strives to create a broader ecosystem to support new moms:

Who Will Take on Her Work? I have been on maternity leave twice (neither employer offered parental leave at the time). I have also had a number of bosses, team members, and peers take leave. When there's no clear plan for transitioning responsibilities or one that simply throws work onto employees and colleagues, it creates a great deal of anxiety. A new mom might feel like she is burdening her team, while her peers become resentful.

One solution is to create a pool of former employees who know your organization well and could consult for a few months to cover the work, or partner with an organization like The Second Shift, founded by Gina Hadley and Jenny Galluzzo, which has created a marketplace to match companies with women experts who can help on certain projects or to cover leaves.[7] This is how my second maternity leave was handled: My boss hired a former employee as a consultant to cover my work for the six months I was out.

If you can't bring in a consultant and need current team members to help, ensure they are compensated with a cash bonus or an increase in base salary. If they don't have bandwidth, consider tapping other people in the organization to help and reward them.

How Will You Assess Her Performance? I once received a poor performance review after I'd just come back from maternity leave. I'd previously been told that I'd met my deliverables and was leaving the team in strong shape, and the rationale for the new rating was vague: "The business is now in decline."

Don't operate this way. Instead, sit down with individuals before they take leave and give them detailed feedback on their performance year-to-date versus their goals. If necessary, explain how the leave will affect any merit or bonus pay. If a formal review would have taken place while they were out, promise another formal review when they return. Some might want to have this conversation during their leave.

If you are forced to rank team members on a "bell curve," evaluate those on parental leave based on their performance before their leave. If you find that new parents are falling to the lower end of the curve, your organization needs to have an open and honest dialogue about the biases you're bringing to the table.

What Are Her Career Aspirations?   When I once raised my hand for a role that would require significant travel, a former boss said to me: "Your kids are too young. You don't want to be on the road and away from them that much." I wasn't given the option to apply; the decision was made for me. For all the times leaders tried to make career decisions for me that they decided were in the best interest of my children, I wish I had asked: Who gave you permission to slow down my career?

Don't assume that new mothers want to be on the "mommy track."[8] Instead, continue to ask about and understand her career aspirations, checking in as you would with any employee on how they want to grow in the organization. Come into those conversations with an open mind and listen carefully.

If you hear that her career aspirations are unchanged, ensure that she is guaranteed her same role when she returns and included in succession planning for key roles. Give her clear guidance on what it takes to get that next assignment or promotion and ask her whether or not she would like to be contacted during her leave about upcoming opportunities.

What Other Policies Do You Have To Support New Mothers? Companies need a robust suite of policies to make motherhood work for new mothers. Consider how you can offer new mothers ways to ramp back to work after they return from leave.

While some women want options to help them ramp back to full-time work, others want to explore alternative options. Offer a suite of possibilities including flexible working, part time, or jobsharing opportunities for all individuals.

Ensure all of your offices have a mother's room, where women can pump comfortably and privately. Consider installing a hospital-grade pump so she can bring in just her pump parts instead of her machine. Design rooms to include comfortable seating, a fridge, a sink, and a microwave. Allowing women who travel for work the benefit of shipping their breast milk home can be a game-changer. Back-up childcare is another key offering, which many companies have added during the pandemic.

Finally, tech companies, including Facebook, Google, and Salesforce, have also started to offer additional paid time off for caregivers.[9] The pandemic has had a devastating impact in particular on mothers in the workplace, creating new challenges and reminding us of obstacles that always existed.[10] There are opportunities for companies to step up and do more, particularly in providing access to childcare facilities either onsite or near the office. Offer caregiver stipends, which can lessen the financial burden and also be used for elder care support, given the rising costs of caregiving.

How Will You Know If You Are Successful? What gets measured gets done. How do you know if you are retaining mothers? Track how many return from leave (and if they don't return, don't assume it's because they don't want to work anymore). Measure how long they stay out after their first child and any subsequent children. Patagonia is a great example of a company that focuses on this data and has strong retention. It supports mothers with policies such as onsite childcare and an organizational culture that embraces rather than ignores employees' families.[11]

2. Do You Really Have Equitable Internal Promotion Processes?

As we discussed at length, helping to eliminate bias in the recruiting process is part of our journey to be more inclusive leaders. It also continues to be a hot topic that gains traction in the marketplace. According to a study by Aptitude Research, 9 out of 10 companies surveyed remained concerned about bias in their recruiting process.[12] And yet, we don't always apply the same level of attention and energy to hiring external talent as we do to internal promotions.

According to McKinsey's Women in the Workplace study, persistent gaps remain in the corporate pipeline for women. The "broken rung"[13] begins at the very first manager level. Women are promoted to manager at much lower rates than men—a trend the study has documented since 2016. Women of color continue to lose ground; between the entry level role and the C-Suite, representation of women of color drops more than 75 percent.

Be sure to consider the following to ensure you are advancing the careers of all women fairly and equitably:

Target Diverse Slates for Promotion

When a promotion opportunity becomes available, stop the leader from just placing someone in the role. Consider all possible candidates across the organization who should be in the running. If you do succession planning for senior roles in collaboration with HR, there will be candidates already identified. And you should post the role internally and externally to cast a wider net. Remember, when focusing on including women on the slate to not only focus on white women, also include women of color.

Forget Mentors; Be a Career Sponsor

When it comes to the promotion process, do you have more men who have career sponsors in the room advocating for their promotions? Do the women who are being considered for promotions have career sponsors? Who is advocating for her career behind closed doors? As we discussed in the previous chapter, forget mentors, be a career sponsor because women don't need more mentors. Ensure women are set up for success with the right advocates in the room when their names come up for promotion opportunities.

Focus on Leadership Performance, Not Potential

When discussing promotions, focus on what the employee's leadership performance has been, not their potential. Too often, I have been in a room when a leader is discussing a woman's candidacy and says, "I am not sure if she has the gravitas for the role" or "I don't think she's likeable enough for the team to follow her" or "She needs to be nicer and more collaborative if she wants to play in the big leagues." When we discuss a woman's leadership potential, negative bias is more likely to creep in. For men, positive bias may creep in "Sure, he's never done that exact job before, and he's up for it" or "I've worked with him for years; the team will rally around him" and "Sure, the promotion may be a stretch, but he has potential. He will rise to the challenge." When it comes to promotions, be clear on what the promotion and new responsibilities entail versus their current role. And focus on leadership performance: metrics and targets achieved; contributions to the team and their organization; their track record of accomplishments. Remember, our job as inclusive leaders is to watch out for and interrupt bias in the workplace.

Watch Out for Biased Language When Evaluating Performance

Ask yourself if you have ever been in a conversation where a woman's performance was being judged using the following language.

- Is she being judgmental or honest?
- Is she being abrasive or direct?
- Is she taking up too much space or expressing her opinion?
- Is she too quiet or being an active listener?
- Is she angry or disagreeing?
- Is she impulsive or decisive?
- Is she too mean/being a bitch or being firm?
- Is she disruptive or a disruptor?
- Is she emotional or passionate?
- Is she not collaborative or taking credit for the impact she made?
- Is she a showoff or has deep expertise?
- Is she a troublemaker or surfacing concerns?
- Is she bossy or leading?
- Is she a pushover or being a team player?
- Is she aloof/cold or is she focused on delivering?
- Is she pushy or assertive?
- Is she difficult or sharing a different opinion?
- Is she not committed to her career? Or is that our perception because she's a mother? Do we question fathers on their commitment to their careers?

Next time this happens, try reframing the question and ask if we would use the same language when evaluating men.

Utilize Gender Appointment Ratio

If you are looking for a way to measure your progress in eliminating bias in your promotion or appointment, consider using the Gender Appointment Ratio (GAR) Metric. At Unilever, they use the GAR metric to provide a track record of promotions to senior leaders.[14] By providing a historical view, you may find patterns and unpack where bias may have come into play in men getting promoted more than women. If you use this metric, be sure to also distinguish promotion rates between white women and women of color. Historically, initiatives in diversity, equity, and inclusion have helped white women while at times excluding women of color. We need to ensure all women are included in our efforts to create more inclusive workplaces for women, and that women of color are not left behind.

Fighting Gendered Ageism

Gendered ageism is the intersection of gender bias and age. Women continue to face the majority of age discrimination in our workplaces for being "too young" or "too old." Age discrimination can seem to be socially acceptable and can be subtle, with jokes about older women not being able to keep up and be tech savvy, or younger women can be dismissed or reduced to how they look. And age discrimination can have a significant impact on women's livelihoods; two years into the pandemic, women over 65 years or older had yet to recover from pandemic-related employment losses.[15]

As women visibly look older, they can be targeted, as in the case of beloved and award-winning Canadian television news

(continued)

(continued)

anchor Lisa LaFlamme. It was widely reported that an executive at LaFlamme's job questioned her decision to let her hair go gray; LaFlamme was abruptly terminated.[16] And according to American Association of Retired Persons (AARP), "81 percent of working women age 50-plus who experience discrimination regularly have felt pressured to look or act a certain way at work."[17] Finally, the research work of Professor David Neumark, an economics professor at the University of California, shows that women face more discrimination than men starting in their 40s: "The evidence of age discrimination against women kind of pops out in every study. Ageism at work begins at 40 for women and 45 for men. At that point, the employer no longer considers the worker for promotion or training."[18]

On our journey to be more inclusive leaders, we must address age discrimination and support women of every age. Here are some ways in which you can help fight gendered ageism in your organization:

- Have you looked at your workforce data (with the help of your legal team) to see how many women versus men over 50 you employ? What patterns do you see?
- Have you looked at your recent layoffs or restructuring (with the help of your legal team) to see how many women versus men over 50 are no longer with the organization? What patterns do you see?
- Have you considered attracting more candidates over 40 (with the help of your legal team) to apply for roles in order to have more generational diversity in your organization?
- When discussing women candidates for roles, have you ever heard the following:

- "I don't know if she will be able to keep up with the pace here."
- "She looks young and sounds young. Clients won't take her seriously."
- "We are a tech company; we can't bring in people who aren't tech savvy."
- "She lacks the professional maturity required for this type of role."
- "We need people who are excited to be here, and she didn't seem very energetic."
- "She seems to have too much experience."
- "She will slow things down for us; it will take too much time to onboard her."

Remember, your job is to interrupt the bias by asking open-ended questions, asking for evidence and facts to back up the statements made, and to ask ourselves if we would make the same statements when evaluating men.

3. Do You Consistently Ask Women What Support They Want and Need?

Remember to always ask what someone wants and needs. Women, like any other group, are not a monolith. Don't come up with solutions if you don't have an understanding of the problems you should help solve. As we discussed before, your positive intent could land with a negative impact.

If you do annual or semi-annual employee surveys, pay special attention to how women are scoring and what their experience is like working in your organization. Host roundtables and listening hours to give them a space to share what they are feeling and experiencing. Don't ignore the data or the insights. I have seen a number of leaders deny, gaslight, or dismiss the experiences women are sharing. Believe the data and believe the stories women share with you. If you don't believe a problem exists, you won't be able to resolve it.

Be open to crowd-sourcing ideas from women to help create solutions. And remember, it is not the job of women and it's not their burden to fix the systems and process that are inequitable and broken. It is the job of us all, it's the job of leadership to fix and, in some cases, rebuild what is broken and be intentional about how we build inclusive cultures.

Supporting women goes beyond a simple extension of maternity leave. We need to support women in every stage of their careers. We need to ensure we interrupt bias and challenge our systems and processes and hold women to the same standards we hold men. On our journey to be more inclusive leaders, we must realize we are responsible for ensuring women stop merely surviving and start thriving in our organizations.

Tips on How Leaders Can Support Women on Their Journey to Motherhood

I worked for organizations who had all of the right policies on paper to support women who were expecting. And yet, none of these policies matter if leaders don't show up for women and support them when they announce their pregnancy and go on leave. Here are tips for leaders on how to support women who are expecting:

Be supportive when an expecting parent announces their pregnancy

"You waited four months to tell me," my boss reprimanded me when I shared my pregnancy news. "You should have told me earlier," she lamented. "We all suspected anyway."

Here's the only response needed: "Congratulations!" Be supportive in the moment. Let's respect the hard choices moms-to-be make about when to tell us about their pregnancies. You don't know the details of their journey to try and become a mother. Also, don't remind them the business is on fire, we have a hiring freeze, or that two other colleagues also just announced their pregnancies. Let pregnancy announcements be about the family, not about the business.

Don't write employees off once they announce their pregnancies

"You will be out on leave when we have the national sales meeting," my boss said, shrugging her shoulders. No need for you to present our innovation plans to the VP of sales."

Months before my due date, I was pulled off major initiatives, taken off meeting invites, and told I no longer needed to present. I remember fighting for the opportunity to be able to present to a major customer while seven months pregnant. The fact that someone is pregnant doesn't mean they can't continue to work and deliver. Don't take opportunities away from expecting parents.

(continued)

Don't pressure employees to work while they are on leave

"Hi, sorry to bother you," the first text began. "I need you to go into the performance review system and enter in ratings for your team, the system won't let me," my boss pleaded. This was a few weeks into my maternity leave. I felt bad, so I did it immediately.

And then the flood gates opened. My boss, and then my temporary backfill, texted me periodically when they needed something. I felt pressured to comply.

Don't pressure employees to work on leave. Reaching out to check-in on how your employees are doing is fine—just don't sneak in a work request (or two or three) while you're doing it.

Have a plan in place for addressing team issues while a manager is on leave

When I came back to work, I came back to six months of unaddressed team performance issues. On my very first day back, I had a meeting with HR to discuss it. My boss's response was, "I waited for you to come back to handle this, I didn't have time." In six months, no proper feedback or coaching was given to team members and an agency relationship had been put on thin ice as a result.

Don't wait for your managers to come back from leave before you address issues. Before they go on leave, make sure there's coverage for their work and duties are delegated appropriately. And if worse comes to worst, higher-level managers need to be willing to step in and address performance issues themselves.

Stop microaggressions against mothers in their tracks

Here's a sample of some of the things I heard when I came back to work after maternity leave:

- "How was your vacation?"
- "Who is home with your baby if you're at work?"
- "You must be working part-time now."
- "My wife stays home because I don't want a nanny raising our children."
- "You decided to come back to work so soon?"

All of the above reveals bias on how we may view women who are working outside the home: That childcare isn't hard work, that you're a bad mother or parent if you return to the workforce, that new parents won't be as committed as they were before.

Stop biased language and everyday microaggressions in its tracks. If we wouldn't ask these questions of fathers, don't ask them of mothers coming back to work after expanding their families. Don't be a silent bystander. Speak up when you hear people asking moms these questions and be the ally that all mothers deserve.

These DEI Efforts Don't Benefit Me. My Voice as a White Man Doesn't Count Anymore.

"These DEI efforts don't benefit me," a white man once said to me during one of our workshops on how to interrupt your bias when evaluating talent. "Sure, I come to these conversations because I have to. But I know the drill, it's usually the white men who are to blame for everything that's gone wrong in our companies."

As we continued our conversation, I asked him why he felt that way. Was there something in the workshop materials or something the facilitator did or said? Did he have feedback on what we could have done differently?

"No one said or did anything that upset me. But I honestly don't even know what to say or do anymore. One time I raised my hand and asked if someone could explain what pronouns were and the woke police came after me," he said. "So I tend to just keep my mouth shut and sit in the back and scroll on my phone. It's clear my voice as a white man doesn't count anymore."

Over the course of my career, I have coached many white men. I still consider many of them to be great leaders, career sponsors, allies in our organizations, and friends who have supported me in the highs and lows of my career. Many of them have started to educate themselves and are more involved in their companies' diversity, equity, and inclusion efforts because they see how much I care. So they are curious to learn and do more. Many of them are motivated to be a more inclusive leader for the women in their lives, friends and colleagues, their wives, their sisters and cousins, and for their daughters. And to be a stronger role model for their sons.

And when it comes to our diversity, equity, and inclusion efforts, here's the one thing not enough of us say aloud: Many white men feel excluded from this work. They don't see the benefits of DEI. They feel alienated, they don't feel like they belong, or that their voice matters anymore.

"Oh, yup, they only promoted her because she's a woman. Need to make those numbers look better."

"No one can make a joke around here anymore. Not since the DEI police arrived. And believe me, they are after the white men."

"They want me to sit in these mandatory trainings so I can feel bad about myself. And I haven't done anything wrong."

"I was going to apply for that role. And my boss said don't waste your time, they are only looking for diverse hires."

"You have to be careful what you do or say—you don't want to be another white guy in the headlines."

"If you say the wrong thing, you are in trouble. If you say nothing, then you are the asshole who said nothing. Straight white guys can't catch a break."

If we want our DEI efforts to be successful, we must debunk this myth. Because we can't do this work without white men. Without white men, we can't change our organizations. We can't change the way we lead, the way we work, or the way we interact with each other. Because in many of our work settings, white men hold more privilege. And with that privilege comes power. The power to help transform our workplaces.

If you are a white man reading this or someone who works with white men, we need to work together to debunk the myth that DEI efforts don't benefit white men. And that their voices don't matter. It's all of our jobs to ensure white men have a seat at the table when it comes to diversity, equity, and inclusion efforts. Here are five ways in which we can ensure white men are included in this work and allow their voices to be heard:

1. Let's Stop Shaming and Blaming White Men

First, let's start by no longer shaming, blaming, demonizing, pointing fingers, or joking about the negative impact white men have in our workplaces. This subtle or overt shaming and blaming can happen in DEI trainings or in one-on-one interactions. As we have learned, stereotypes can be incredibly damaging. Shattering stereotypes must also include, and not exclude, what we think about white men. That only white men can be racist or sexist or homophobic. That their privilege, when it comes to gender and race, makes them solely responsible for all of the things going wrong in our workplaces, in our communities, and in the greater world. These stereotypes can prevent us from including and building bridges with white men.

Blaming or guilting white men only builds up walls and creates further division. And we need them to be part of co-creating solutions and be committed to this work.

"Oh, come on, he's a white man. He won't understand where I am coming from, we have nothing in common," a woman of color once said to me. She was interested in applying for a role in Finance. I encouraged her to go and meet with one of the Directors, who was a white man. She convinced herself he wouldn't be interested in meeting with her and they had nothing in common. Why would a white man open doors and opportunities for her?

"How would you feel if someone judged you based on how you looked, or based on a story they had created about you in their head without ever talking with you?" I asked her.

"Well," she paused, reflecting on my question. "I hadn't thought about it that way."

She finally agreed to meet with him, so I made the introduction. And over time, this became one of the best career sponsorship relationships I had the privilege to watch grow. She later acknowledged she was wrong in making assumptions about him without getting to know him first. She judged him incorrectly because, as she said, "he was a white man."

If you are a white man reading this, remember to extend the same kindness and grace you would want others to give to you when building relationships. As discussed before, building relationships takes time and effort, and we will make mistakes—we will make assumptions, create false narratives, and knowingly or unknowingly hold on to stereotypes. We must make an effort to forgive and move forward in relationships when it comes to making progress in DEI (we will cover more on the importance of apologies and what we can learn from them later).

2. Help Educate White Men on the Statistics

"As a middle-aged white man, it's tough out there," a white leader said to me. "We are being ignored and left behind. We are the dinosaurs on the verge of extinction; there aren't too many of us left."

For white men to be invested in DEI efforts, we must start by educating them on the statistics, so they can begin to understand the privilege they in fact do hold. According to a *New York Times* study, 80 percent of the "faces of power" are white, and mostly white men. This study includes the most powerful people in the United States, who "pass our laws, run Hollywood's studios, and head the most prestigious universities. They own pro sports teams and determine who goes to jail and who goes to war."[1] Of the Fortune 500 companies CEOs, 85 percent of them are men. In one *Fortune* survey of 16 Fortune 500 companies, it was revealed that white men account for 72 percent of corporate leadership.[2] Finally, a study done during the pandemic showed that men were promoted three times more than women when so many businesses shut down and layoffs occurred.[3]

This means for white men that they are more than fairly represented in the institutions, systems, and processes that make decisions on their behalf and ensure they are included. To make it more personal, share with white men your organization's workforce data and insights. Who is leading some of your biggest businesses? Who is sitting in the C-Suite? Who is getting promoted the fastest, getting paid more, and has access to informal and formal career sponsors?

Use the data to help change the narrative they may believe about being left behind. We want white men to understand that DEI efforts are not about a zero-sum game where one person losing means another person is winning. There isn't one pie with a limited number of slices. As the pie grows and more pies are added, as we invest more in DEI efforts, we will see more business opportunities open up. Finally, there needs to be acknowledgment that many of our systems and processes in our organizations never started from a place of fairness. So when I talk to white men who say, "I am all for fairness, and may the best person get the job," I work with them to acknowledge and understand the statistics. And accept that our leaders and organizations haven't always operated from a place of fairness. You have to acknowledge there is a problem before you are willing to fix it. And we need white men to understand they can use their power and influence to be more inclusive leaders and to help build more inclusive workplaces.

3. Create Spaces for White Men to Learn and Grow Together

No matter who you are, you want to feel like you belong, that you have a place in your organization, and that you matter. It's hard to feel included if you feel blamed for things you didn't do or don't understand what you did wrong; if you are shamed for asking questions you don't know the answers to; if you are silenced when you make a mistake; if you continue to be under attack and your apology is not accepted; if you are overcome by fear, worried about doing the wrong thing, and so instead you choose to do nothing.

We must invite white men into this work. In my experience, one-on-one coaching, sharing, and learning about each other's lived experiences and intimate group-based discussions can all create a safe space for men to grow and learn. Remember, we don't want to force, push, or shame anyone into doing this work. In many companies I have worked with, Men as Allies spaces are being formed. In some cases, DEI teams are helping to lead these spaces. In other cases, white men leaders are forming Men as Allies ERGs to convene men on how they can grow and learn together. A first step can be to host a closed-door session for men only, led by an outside, preferably a man who is a skilled facilitator, a member of the DEI team, or a leader who understands the importance of DEI and wants to facilitate. Because white men may feel more comfortable in this space learning from other men. This should be a space where they can ask questions or share any stories or observations without judgment. The key is to have someone skilled in the room, leading the discussion, answering questions, and helping educate the men.

In many of these spaces, you will hear men opening up about their own struggles: becoming a father for the first time, having to care for their own father, the stress to provide for their own family, the pressure to conform to our society's "masculine" standards, the inability to show emotion, the racism men of color continue to face, suffering from burnout, and more. Men in our workplaces need to take care of themselves before they can show up and be there for others.

According to a U.S. national study "What Majority Men Really Think About Diversity and Inclusion," majority men were categorized into three personas: Detractors, Persuadables, and True Believers. The Detractors were the smallest group (about 10 percent of the sample) and believed DEI was not important at all. Persuadables said DEI was "not very" or "somewhat" important (48 percent of the sample). Finally, True Believers said DEI was "very or extremely important" (42 percent of the sample) and were likely to be the most involved. The area of opportunity lies in spending time converting more Persuadables into True Believers and getting True Believers to put their beliefs into practice and show their commitment.[4]

True inclusion is about including all voices. We don't shut out voices because they have a differing opinion or because we assume they won't want to learn or grow. With Detractors, a small percentage may be able to move to Persuadables and then ultimately become True Believers. But that doesn't mean we continue to include voices who actively hurt and harm others, with no signs of remorse or willingness to change. Some detractors will fall into this category, and we can't continue to have them take up space if they are not interested in changing. As discussed earlier, these individuals ultimately must move on to their next chapter outside of our organizations and seek out therapy to start their own healing journey so that they stop inflicting repeated pain onto others.

How "Men as Allies" Movements Can Be Successful in Your Organization

When I was first starting my work in the DEI field, my friend Carol Watson introduced me to Chuck Shelton of Great Heart Consulting. Chuck and I have partnered a number of times over the years, specifically on "White Men as Inclusive Leaders." Chuck and his team boldly say, "We don't believe white guys are fragile or broken or that they need to be fixed. We don't believe positional authority is a corruptor, but rather an opportunity."[5]

Chuck reminds me that white men already possess many traits required to commit to DEI: They want to beat competition; they want to generate value, they want to lead great teams, and they want to become great leaders. For white men interested in learning more about the work Chuck Shelton has been leading, read his book: *Leadership 101 for White Men*. Suggesting this book to some of the white men in your organization is a good first step, before they start to form a "Men as Allies" movement. Invite a handful of men to read the book and have them recommend it to other colleagues so that they can start to influence each other on the importance of this work.

Here are tips on setting up a successful "Men as Allies" movement:

- Find senior white men who want to sponsor this work and will commit to being visible. Ask them to help fund this work. Invite them to announce to the organization that they are leading this and ask them to personally invite men they know to get involved.
- Bring in skilled facilitators or ask your DEI team for help on how to host a first discussion on engaging white men.
- Ensure the group is open to all men. While the majority may be white men, pay particular attention to the voices of men of color. As we discussed earlier, in women's initiatives women of color are often left behind. Ensure men of color feel comfortable to participate.
- Ask the men to come up with an annual action plan, including books and articles to read, hosting smaller group coaching circles, bringing in external speakers, having an accountability partner, co-hosting community conversations with other ERGs, and sharing their commitments on how they will show up differently at work.

If you choose to formalize this as an ERG, remember our prior discussion. It's not the job of the ERGs to run the DEI strategy. Ensure the DEI team is involved. And ensure there is budget available to support this work.

4. Show White Men the Benefits of Diversity, Equity, and Inclusion Efforts

When leaders and organizations fully embrace DEI efforts, you will have a more diverse workforce. You will be on your journey to build more inclusive leaders and, as a result, a more inclusive culture. You will have fair and equitable systems and processes. You will outperform your competition who don't embrace DEI as a competitive advantage.

Here are three ways to show white men the benefits of DEI:

The Business Case

- Diverse Teams Perform Better: According to a McKinsey study, "companies in the top quartile for ethnic and cultural diversity outperform those in the fourth quartile by 36 percent.[6] Companies in the top quartile for gender diversity on executive teams were 25 percent more likely to have above-average profitability than companies in the fourth quartile."[7] And the greater the representation, the higher the likelihood of outperformance.
- Narrowing the Gender Gap: $12 trillion in additional GDP if gender gap is narrowed by 2025.[8]
- Tapping the Spending Power of the Multicultural Consumer: According to Nielsen, this combined spending power of Black/African American, Asian Americans, and Hispanics/Latinos is $3.2 trillion.[9] This translates into opportunities for more innovation and more ways to serve and connect these communities with products and services. This translates into more growth and more revenue for your organization.

The Case for Attracting and Retaining Talent

- According to a Glassdoor study, "more than 3 out of 4 job seekers and employees (76 percent) report that a diverse workforce is an important factor when evaluating companies and job offers."[10] The study also notes how important DEI efforts are to those from historically marginalized communities, "Nearly a third of employees and job seekers (32 percent) would not apply for a job at a company where there is a lack of diversity among its workforce."

- According to an Employee Benefits News Study, "the average cost of losing an employee is a staggering 33 percent of their annual salary."[11] And in another study, Black employees were 30 percent more likely to resign than their white colleagues.[12] Yet another reminder that building diverse teams is not enough; you need leaders who are are skilled at leading inclusively.

- According to Udemy, "nearly half of employees said they've quit a job because of a bad manager. What's more, 56 percent think managers are promoted prematurely, and 60 percent think managers need managerial training."[13] This is yet another data point making the case for up-skilling all of our employees to be more inclusive leaders.

The Case for Being a DEI Champion

Finally, the case for white men being DEI champions includes generating differentiated business results and being known for attracting and retaining talent. Additionally, many of the systems, processes, and policies intended to help other employees will likely help white men as well, as evidenced by "The Curb-Cut Effect."[14]

In 1972, faced with pressure from activists advocating for individuals with disabilities, the city of Berkeley, California, installed its first official "curb cut" at an intersection on Telegraph Avenue. In the words of a Berkeley advocate, "the slab of concrete heard 'round the world."[15] This not only helped people in wheelchairs. It also helped parents pushing strollers, elderly with walkers, travelers wheeling luggage, workers pushing heavy carts, and the curb cut helped skateboarders and runners. People went out of their way and continue to do so, to use a curb cut. "The Curb Cut Effect" shows us that one action targeted to help a community ended up helping many more people than anticipated. So in our workplaces, parental leave policies, caregiver support, and flexible workplace policies will also have a ripple effect and help support white men.

And as we discussed earlier when it came to being a sponsor, those who sponsor the career of others will be more likely to rapidly advance in their own careers. Being a visible DEI champion is not only good for your organization but is good for your own career. Investing in DEI efforts is also an investment in your leadership trajectory and a way to differentiate yourself from your peer set.

5. Give White Men Concrete Ways to Help

In my time coaching white men, once they understand and commit to DEI efforts, they ask me for concrete ways to help. As we end this section, I have compiled a list of ways white men can help, including some areas we have already discussed. Our current way of working and building our organizations can't change without the help of white men. We need as many white men as possible showing up as inclusive leaders and understanding, yes, they have a place in this work.

Tips for White Men on How to Start Committing to DEI Efforts

1. Start with role-modeling inclusive leadership behaviors. Hold your team members accountable for how they lead and interact with their colleagues.
2. Commit to educating yourself on language. Remember that language matters and is also always evolving. When it doubt, ask for help.
3. Make a public pledge to build a more diverse team also with a focus on women of color. It doesn't matter how big or small your team is—you can commit to changing the diversity of representation of your team. And influence others to do the same.

4. Invest dollars from your budget in external organizations for access to diverse talent pools. Second Shift, Society of Women Engineers, National Society of Black Engineers, Financial Women's Association, and Hispanic Alliance for Career Advancement are a few places to start. Invest your dollars with these organizations to build long-term partnerships.

5. Actively work with recruiting to target diverse slates for open roles and challenge teams to hire the right person for the right role. Work with recruiters and hiring managers to push through bias in hiring caregivers, particularly mothers, if there are gaps on their resume.

6. If you lead a team, ensure all of your employees are paid fairly and equitably. If you don't lead a team, advocate as well for colleagues to ensure they are compensated for their worth.

7. Sponsor women. Use your political capital to help advance her career. Introduce her to other senior leaders. Get her on that taskforce. Put her name on the slate for a role she wasn't even on the radar for. Give her the access. And make sure to sponsor white women and women of color.

8. Fight for policies that impact us all: paid parental leave, mother's rooms, in vitro fertilization and egg freezing medical coverage, financial assistance for adoption, Milk Stork, phased back-to-work programs for new parents, offering resources to deal with teenage cyber bullying, job share opportunities, remote working, and much more.

9. Encourage women and men to take paid parental leave. Set the example. If you have the opportunity, take paid parental leave as well and take the whole time off. Studies show that fathers who take leave help their families and themselves

(continued)

and help set the tone for shared parenting responsibilities at home from the start.[16] Create a culture that supports men taking leave, and an environment where leave doesn't negatively affect promotions.

10. Help fathers reintegrate back into the workplace after taking leave. Encourage them to role-model leaving early for kids' doctor appointments and school activities and adopting flexible ways of working.

11. Decline panel invitations where only men are panelists and demand women be included. Give up your spot to make the point. Also, it's *not* enough if only *white* women are included.

12. As you continue to do the work to educate yourself, be active on LinkedIn and social channels. Share your views by posting articles, commenting, liking, sharing. Don't be a silent advocate. Show us and the rest of the world you really are a DEI champion.

13. Build a Men as Allies initiative, reviewing the steps we outlined earlier to consider what would work in your organization. Be sure to include the voices of men of color and make it a point to learn about their lived experiences. Just like all women are not the same, the same is true for men.

14. Attend Employee Resource Group events and try to bring at least three men with you. Show up. Be present. Engage. Be consistent with your attendance throughout the year.

15. Ask to be one of the Executive Sponsors for your company's women's ERG, Black ERG, AAPI ERG, or a community where you want to understand more about their lived experiences. Sign up to host and fund events out of your budget.

16. Interrupt bias when you see it in action. "She should smile more." "She lacks gravitas." "She is bossy and aggressive."

"She can't keep up with the pace here." "She lacks potential for this role." Ask yourself—would you use that language to describe a man? As we discussed before, it's never too late to educate and do the right thing, even after the moment has passed.

17. Support women-owned businesses and founders of color by supporting them and buying from them (consider thank you gifts or holiday gifts for your team).

18. Think of the role your organization can play in creating fair and equitable processes in the greater ecosystem. Companies like Chobani, Diageo, Disney, and more have accelerators to help entrepreneurs from historically marginalized groups start their own companies.[17] It's an opportunity to lift up and support founders starting the next generation of game-changing companies.

19. Stop bullying and harassment in its tracks. Don't be that leader who says or does nothing. And don't be that leader who waits for HR to jump in. Be the leader we *need* you to be.

20. Finally, find at least one other man in your workplace to join you in this work. Ask him to do the above and continue to ask other men to join you in DEI efforts.

No One Can Question Our Support of the LGBTQ+ Community. Look at How Much Money We Invest in June Pride Month! We Aren't Diversity Washers.

"No one can question our support of the LGBTQ+ community," a former leader shouted at me. "Look at how much money we invest in June Pride Month!"

This was after I presented a proposal to him and other leaders with inputs from our PRIDE Employee Resource Group (ERG) on the ways in which the company could have more inclusive benefits. The proposal included additional financial support for adoption and surrogacy, health care coverage for gender affirmation surgery, and most importantly, ensuring health care benefits to domestic partners of employees. One of the brands showed lavish external support of June Pride Month, including hosting pricey external events during the month of June and participating in a local Pride parade with an extravagant float. This raised questions for the members of our LGBTQ+ community on what the company overall was doing to support the internal community.

"Well, the members of the ERG feel that is rainbow washing, a form of diversity washing. They feel we could re-invest those dollars into more meaningful efforts for our employees. And that we . . ."

"Why are we even talking about this?" He interrupted me, growing more irritated. "What happened to the proposal I asked you about? Launching one of our products with the rainbow flavor? Just like Doritos did, that's what we should be focusing on. We need to capitalize on this moment," he reprimanded me. He opened his desk drawer and tossed an old bag of Doritos at me that had rainbow flavors. I caught the bag and stared at purple, blue, green, orange, and red chips displayed on the bag. The pressure to participate in rainbow washing was on.

One of the myths many leaders continue to cling to was incredibly well articulated by this former leader: *No one can question our support of the LGBTQ+ community. Look at how much money we invest in June Pride Month.* Because most of us don't want to believe or accept that we may be diversity washing.

Unfortunately, too many leaders I have worked with over the years believe the easy shortcut to inclusion is showing up in the external marketplace with a tweet, an Instagram image with a rainbow, a fancy press release, a one-time non-profit donation, an endorsement from a TikTok influencer, or a rainbow-flavored product to show that we are allies. We support the LGBTQ+ community. Of course, we are allies. The question is, are you only allies in the month that matters like Pride? And as we discussed before, you can't just self-appoint yourself as an ally. Would your LGBTQ+ employees say you are allies for them year-round?

The pressure to show up, speak up, and be loud during heritage months and cultural and religious moments continues to intensify in our current digital age where you are simply one post, one like, or one click away from showing up as an ally:

> "It's Black History Month. Should we ask the Black Associate on the Finance Team to post something about how she likes working here?"
>
> "It's Women's International Day. Don't forget to talk about all of our expanded benefits for mothers."
>
> "What's the hashtag for Hispanic Heritage Month again? Or should we translate it into Spanish?"
>
> "Why didn't we post a message on Instagram wishing everyone a Happy Ramadan? Every other brand is doing it and a senior leader is asking me why we haven't posted anything yet."
>
> "We created a campaign with influencers around Asian Pacific Islander Heritage Month. And we just got blasted by the AAPI ERG for not saying anything about Asian hate crimes. I tell you, absolutely zero gratitude."

One of the biggest mistakes we make is not realizing this: our employees are our forgotten consumers. We spend so much time thinking about the external marketplace, obsessing over who we can sell our products and services to, how fast, and how much we can make. We don't actually take the time to ask ourselves how our employees feel about how we are selling, and how we are positioning ourselves as an ally in the marketplace. Do we really care about the community or are our actions performative and fleeting? What is our internal track record of supporting this community? Have we even stopped to ask our employees what they think before that campaign goes live?

What Is Rainbow Washing?

According to Urban dictionary, rainbow washing is "the act of using or adding rainbow colors and/or imagery to advertising, apparel, accessories, landmarks, et cetera, in order to indicate progressive support for LGBTQ equality (and earn consumer credibility)—but with a minimum of effort or pragmatic result. (It is akin to "green-washing" with environmental issues and "pink-washing" with breast cancer.)"[1] Rainbow washing, or Pride washing, primarily occurs during June Pride month, which is celebrated annually to honor the 1969 Stonewall riots. This moment marked the beginning of a movement to end discriminatory laws and practices against the LGBTQ+ community.

Gilbert Barker, an activist and artist, designed the rainbow Pride Flag in 1978. Barker was inspired by the symbolic significance of rainbows throughout history and selected each color to have a specific meaning.[2] The rainbow Pride Flag represents the diversity of the community and has become a symbol the whole community can embrace and rally around.

For organizations, rainbow washing can come off as performative allyship or performative activism. The intention is to gain attention for yourself or others. And to make money off the community or the cause. It's done without having the right intention: to make a difference, to uplift and actually serve the community.

As I have worked with leaders, here are some of the types of rainbow washing (or June Pride washing) I have seen. If you scroll on your phone, walk down the aisles of stores, or watch what's happening during Pride month in your organization, you may observe or witness firsthand some of the following:

- Applying rainbows to social media posts or email signatures or changing the brand or company logo to rainbow colors only for the month of June (as opposed to having a Pride Flag hanging in your office, placed in your email signature, or as part of your virtual background 365 days a year).
- Pressuring LGTBQ+ employees to be featured in social media campaigns or using their images without their permission, and they later discover the use of their images in social media posts.
- Selling rainbow limited edition products with rainbow packaging or rainbow flavors.
- Profiting from rainbow or Pride merchandise and not donating proceeds back to organizations that are trying to uplift and support the community.
- Asking LGBTQ+ influencers to work free for "brand exposure" or drastically underpaying them what their contributions are worth.

This can cause further harm or damage when the lived experience of your LGBTQ+ employees internally doesn't match your external image. This can include LGBTQ+ employees not feeling included or safe in your organizations and not

(continued)

(continued)

having access to inclusive benefits. For some LGBTQ+ employees, they may see all of this external imagery and campaigning for June Pride, but they also know that their organizations are funding Political Action Committees (PACs) that support anti-LGBTQ+ legislation. Disney is an example of this, which we will discuss more in-depth as a case study.

What Is Diversity Washing?

In addition to pride washing, we also see more broadly diversity washing. Our social media feeds continue to be flooded by organizations and brands celebrating Black History Month, Hispanic Heritage Month, Asian Pacific Islander Heritage Month, Indigenous People's Day, Women's International Day, and many more moments. And yet many of these brands are not doing the work necessary to support historically marginalized communities with their wallets. This includes launching a supplier diversity program, partnering with funding grassroots organizations, and finally, hiring, developing, and sponsoring talent from historically marginalized communities on their teams.

This is called diversity washing: externally pushing out DEI statements and goals, rushing to stand up for social justice issues, and celebrating cultural moments that matter while not doing any of the actual work needed. If your employees are surprised by what your brands are saying and doing externally, then that's a red flag and a sign of diversity washing. As discussed, our employees are often our forgotten consumers; before rushing to make external statements, ask for their assessment on where you truly are on your DEI journey.

Leaders are under pressure to find growth. It can be easy to just follow the dollar signs when businesses are stagnant, struggling to capture single-digit growth, and under pressure to continue to find new streams of revenue. According to LGBT Capital, the global purchasing power of the LGBTQ+ community is estimated to be $3.7 trillion; in the United States, the purchasing power of the LGBTQ+ community is estimated to be $900 million.[3] And remember that this purchasing power is available 365 days a year—not just in the month of June.

"Retailers realize and understand that the 'pink dollar' is good money to have coming into the story regularly, not just during Pride Month," said Simon Fenwick, executive vice president of talent and inclusion at the American Association of Advertising Agencies.[4]

"The community and their extended families have become good and loyal customers and so, beyond wanting to do good, businesses are seeing that they have long-term, valuable customers in the LGBT community," Fenwick continued. While some organizations are showing up for the LGBTQ+ community in the right way, some unfortunately continue to get it wrong.

As leaders, before we rush to show up, speak, and be loud for heritage months and cultural and religious moments, let's stop and pause. We must go beyond the rainbows in June. This isn't a check the box exercise or the one time to speak to a community. It should be the beginning of the journey to amplify, celebrate, honor, connect, and advocate for a community. Here are four questions to ask ourselves to ensure this intentional act of inclusion doesn't end after "the month" is over:

Do You Understand the Issues Facing the Community?

Before rushing to celebrate and capitalize on these months, do you have an understanding of what issues the community is facing? As discussed earlier, do you understand what your intent is and what you want your impact to be? Are you working on this in a silo, on your own, with access to limited voices or restricting access for more voices to be included? Who is on the core team working on the broader campaign, the product launch, or the specific content you are creating? Finally, are we creating something for a community without their voices being represented and listened to at the table?

As leaders, we must be humble enough to speak up when there is something we don't have the answer to or we don't understand. As we discussed earlier, our job on our journey to be more inclusive leaders is to build empathy and understanding for experiences that are not our own. And if we are pressuring our teams or feeling pressured to participate in this monthly moment, we must stop and ask ourselves why. As a Black colleague once said to me in response to what she thought was a company's performative Black History Month activities, "I am Black 365 days a year, not just Black in the month of February."

Have You Asked Your Employees How They Feel?

One of the biggest misses I have witnessed is leaders rushing to launch a big external campaign for June Pride month, with only a limited number of employees seeing it in advance. And in many cases, none of these employees identify as LGBTQ+. Remember, it does not mean it's the burden of your employees to call out if they think a campaign or product idea is racist, sexist, homophobic, hurtful, or harmful to a particular community. Just because they belong to that particular community doesn't mean that they represent the entire community. It is an important moment to ask if they would like to be included before it comes up on their social feeds.

In this case, there may be an opportunity for Employee Resource Groups to partner with you on this work. We will discuss more later on how to ensure your ERGs are not being tokenized, used, or bearing the burden of driving your organization's DEI work. Outside of ERGs, you can also ask employees to raise their hand to volunteer to give feedback and be involved, in which case, you should pay them for their time just like you would with external consumers. Or offer to make a donation instead to a nonprofit serving the community you are striving to be an ally for. Having access to voices of the community you are serving is critical. We will discuss this further when we address setting up inclusion ecosystems when it comes to marketing.

Do You Have Inclusive Benefits for the LGBTQ+ Community?

Before you show up for the LGBTQ+ community externally, you must assess the internal experience of your LGBTQ+ employees. One place to start is ask yourself if you have inclusive benefits for the LGBTQ+ community. Here's a starting list to consider, adapted from the Human Rights Campaign Foundation (HRC) including:

- Inclusive benefits for same and different sex spouses and partners (including family planning and financial planning)
- Transgender-inclusive health care coverage, including but not limited to "mental health, pharmacy benefits for hormone therapy, medical visits and lab procedures related to hormone therapy, surgical procedures, and short-term leave for surgical procedures."[5]
- Gender transition/affirmation guidelines to proactively support, first and foremost, the transitioning employee, as well as their leaders and their teams.

(continued)

(*continued*)

Finally, remember, you can't create inclusive benefits for your LGBTQ+ employees without their input and giving them a seat at the table as you embark on this work. Ensure the community is included early enough in the journey to provide adequate input and to feel that they are part of this work. For a detailed list of comprehensive benefits, and for further educational resources, please visit the Human Rights Campaign Foundation.

Is Your Brand or Company the Right Ally?

In some cases, we have to understand and acknowledge that you are not the right ally. If you aren't the right ally yet, please don't force it. You must be ready to go beyond a token gesture. Here are some examples to consider:

- You have little to no Black representation at your small company. Instead of posting a square on Instagram saying, "Celebrating Black History Month," you can use this as an internal opportunity to educate non-Black leaders on how they could be a better ally to the Black community. And how leaders can come together to attract and retain more Black talent.
- You want to sign an external pledge on pay equity for International Women's Day, but you have no plans to talk to your employee base about your compensation philosophy. Or to disclose if women are being paid fairly and equitably in comparison to men.
- You planned an AAPI Heritage Month beauty influencer campaign for May, hiring AAPI content creators for this new product launch. Yet, you have not addressed your Asian employees' growing concerns on their feeling unsafe traveling to the office with the rising number of anti-Asian hate crimes in the United States.

- You would like employees and customers to sign a petition for the CROWN act[6] during Black History Month, a movement to end race-based hair discrimination in our workplaces and schools. And yet, you haven't addressed the discrimination your Black employees have faced, being told to wear their hair "more professionally" to work.

- You are posting about celebrating and honoring "Indigenous People's Day," but the company still has standing Friday team meetings called "pow-wows" and for the company's last Halloween party, someone dressed as an "Indian" won best prize. Remember that someone else's race and culture is not a costume.

If this is your first time participating in a cultural or heritage moment, be intentional and do the work slowly. Don't look at May, Asian Pacific Island Heritage Month, as the one time to do something. Look at it as the moment to start something and keep the conversation and dialogue going year-round. Lean on external partners; grassroots organizations and larger, more established nonprofits; for-profit partners; and community activists and influencers to help you in this work. Share the spotlight and shine the spotlight brightly on them. Visibly let the community know who you are partnering with; this will make your work all the more meaningful, authentic, and credible. Don't bury it in an asterisk on the product packaging or on a website.

Why Don't You Just Sit This One Out?

Finally, sometimes, it's best just to sit it out. Wait until you are ready. Don't give into the pressure of participating, showing up, honoring, or celebrating a heritage month or an important cultural moment if you aren't equipped to do so. Wait for the right moment to showcase your organization's authentic commitment to serving and being an ally to the community you want to show up for.

If you are feeling pressure to participate, is it pressure you are putting on yourself or it is coming from another leader? Because without preparation, planning, and putting work into this, you may do more harm than good. Convince others to start now doing the work for next year. There's no time like the present to start doing the work now with your employees internally before you race to the marketplace.

Lessons in Allyship from the World of Disney

I have long admired the progress Disney has made when it comes to its diversity, equity, and inclusion efforts. Disney's content has come a long way since I was a little Brown girl watching white princesses on the big screen. Disney now includes a content warning,[7] an explanation for racism that shows up in classic films. They now have gender inclusive costumes for theme park staff,[8] and during the recent Christmas holiday, Black Santas appeared in their parks for the first time ever.[9] And while their Rainbow Disney Collection celebrates the LGBTQ+ community, the headlines show there's more work to be done.[10]

A growing number of Disney employees and fans have felt betrayed by the company's stance on 2022 legislation in Florida, dubbed by advocates as the "Don't Say Gay" bill. Employees organized a walkout and listed their demands to the company, including asking Disney to stop making political donations to certain Florida politicians.[11] While former Disney CEO Bob Chapek did issue an apology, saying he should have been a "stronger ally in the fight for equal rights,"[12] some employees felt like it was too late.

Leaders can begin by asking themselves these three questions to understand what it truly means to be an ally for the LGBTQ+ Community:

1. Do you know what political action committees your company is funding?

Start by educating yourself on what a political action committee (PAC) is,[13] and if your company supports and funds any PACs. A PAC is created to raise and spend money to help get candidates elected and to defeat opponents. In the case of Disney, employees are demanding that Disney "must immediately and indefinitely cease all campaign donations to the politicians involved in the creation or passage of the 'don't say gay' bill."[14] If you are on a journey to be an ally to the LGBTQ+ Community, for example, you can't claim to be an ally and at the same time fund anti-LGBTQ+ legislation. Do your homework and partner with your Corporate Communications and Government Affairs teams to understand where your company stands on social justice and human rights issues.

2. Is your content truly inclusive of the community you claim to be an ally for?

According to a recent study from GLAAD, a media advocacy group, Walt Disney Studios has the weakest history when it comes to LGBTQ inclusion in content.[15] Disney has attempted to make strides with its feature film *Onward*, featuring an openly LGBTQ character. The *LA Times* said it's time for Disney to move beyond token LGBTQ inclusion given that this character's sexuality is only mentioned in passing.[16] And finally, a letter from Pixar employees alleges that Disney corporate executives have cut "nearly every moment of overtly gay affection . . . regardless of when there is protest from both the creative teams and executive

(continued)

(*continued*)

leadership at Pixar."[17] If your company produces any type of content, you have the responsibility and power to shatter stereotypes.

We know that stories have the ability to inspire change, particularly in the case of Disney for young audiences who eagerly watch. It's easy to sell a collection of Rainbow products,[18] and it's another thing to ensure that LGBTQ+ characters and stories are accurately and meaningfully included.

3. Do you truly understand the experience of your employees?

Finally, be weary of chasing external awards that may not truly reflect the experience of your employees. At the beginning of 2022, the Disney company announced that for the sixteenth year in a row it received a score of 100[19] on the Human Rights Campaign (HRC) Foundation's Corporate Equality Index, the nation's foremost benchmarking survey and report measuring corporate policies and practices related to LGBTQ+ workplace equality. And yet Disney employees have mobilized, demanding that Disney do better, and be better, when it comes to allyship for the LGBTQ+ community. Now even the HRC refuses to accept any money from Disney in its efforts to protect LGBTQ+ rights, until the company takes "meaningful action" against Florida's "Don't Say Gay" legislation.[20]

This case study of Disney reminds us of the importance of showing up for our employees in the moments that matter most. When you don't, they can become your harshest critics, walking out the door and sharing with others their experiences. Ultimately, this negatively impacts your employer brand.

And when you do show up for them, they will in turn become your company's fiercest and most loyal supporters.

While we have talked about many of the missteps that can occur during June Pride, there are a number of organizations showing up as an ally to the LGBTQ+ community. Here are some important examples to consider. I encourage you to dive deeper into what these organizations and others are doing—to study their journey to be an ally:

- Getty Images: In collaboration with GLAAD, offered a global creative grant of $25,000 focused on the Chosen Family. The purpose of the grant is to support photographers and videographers to help increase visibility of the LGBTQ+ community while challenging harmful stereotypes.[21]
- Harry's: Introduced the Shave with Pride Set with 100 percent of profits being donated to LGBTQ+ causes. They use the power of their platforms to feature inspiring individuals in the LGBTQ+ community to share their stories.[22]
- The Coca-Cola Company: One of the first U.S. organizations to publicly support the Employment Non-Discrimination Act, alongside 379 businesses to file an amicus brief with the Supreme Court in support of marriage equality. They launched the "Next Generation LGBTQ+ Leaders' Initiative," designed to connect, educate, and inspire young LGBTQ+ leaders to advance the community across all industries.[23]
- IBM: In 1996, IBM was the largest organization to start providing benefits for domestic partners in support of its LGBTQ+ employees.[24]

The pressure to make progress on your DEI journey will only continue to intensify. And remember that writing one-time checks, posting images and inspirational quotes in social media, and other acts of performative allyship and diversity washing will do more harm than good. There are no quick fixes or shortcuts in this work. It's up to each of us to show up as inclusive leaders, ensuring this work is done thoughtfully and consistently on behalf of all our organizations.

Tips on How Leaders Can Set Up ERGs for Success

"How many ERGs do you have? We have 14!"

This is usually the question I am met with when asked about DEI strategies. And a quick, unsolicited response about how many Employee Resource Groups, or ERGs, they have. It always seems to come back to the ERGs, how many there are, and a few quick stories about events they have hosted. I said it before and I will say it again: ERGs are not your DEI strategy.

Of course ERGs should have a place in your organization and in your overall DEI strategy. And here are ways to ensure you are not using, tokenizing, or taking for granted the work of your employees leading your ERGs:

• Ensure they have a designated budget or have access to the DEI budget. Do not make them plan events and then expect them to run around the organization begging for funding. Be equitable about distributing the budget among ERGs.

• Appoint a leader (preferably at C–Suite level or no more than two levels below) to be the Executive Sponsor of the ERG. That Executive Sponsor should also use their own budget to help fund events and drive attendance. This individual doesn't have to identify as part of that ERG. In fact, appointing a leader who is on a journey to be an ally for that community can be powerful. Hold them accountable for being an Executive Sponsor for putting this in their annual performance goals.

• Appoint leaders of the ERG who are on track for internal promotion. Make sure they, and their bosses, know this is an appointment by the company and a leadership opportunity to influence and manage stakeholders and drive a key initiative on behalf of the company. Ensure their goals for the ERG are also embedded in their annual performance goals.

- Embed the work of ERG leaders into their performance goals. The Executive Sponsor should send feedback to the manager when it's time for annual performance reviews. Consider including ERG leaders as part of a formal sponsorship program.
- Compensate ERG leaders. LinkedIn pays ERG leaders $10,000, as do other companies.[25] For too long, individuals leading ERGs have been burdened with additional office work. They need to be rewarded and recognized.
- Ensure ERGs are supported to help drive engagement and create a sense of belonging. It is not their job to educate about DEI. For example, don't ask your Black ERG to host a session on "How to be an Ally to the Black Community." Don't ask an ERG to host "Unconscious Bias" training or best practices on how to interview inclusively. That's not their job. As a leader, that's your job to drive the DEI work and to also make sure you have a DEI team in place to help. If ERGs do ask to help co-lead an event, ensure they are an equal partner and are truly co-leading the work versus asking them to then do all the work and lead it.
- Do not put pain on display. Do not gather your ERG members in response to another Black man being killed by police, an Asian woman being attacked on the subway, or a hate crime against the LGBTQ+ community so that everyone else can sob, stare, and listen to their stories. As discussed before, don't inflict further pain on individuals who have already been harmed by putting them on the spot to share their stories.

(*continued*)

- Don't force ERGs into existence. It's not a race to see how many ERGs you have to prove how inclusive you are. Start small and see how they grow. Encourage and support growth of ERGs; don't make anyone ever feel guilty for not leading an ERG.
- Don't pressure, require, or mandate ERGs to host and drive engagement during cultural moments and heritage months.
- Evolve ERGs into Business Resource Groups. This means giving them goals that can help serve the business. This could be helping start an internship program with recruiting, co-leading a new product or a service with engineering, or co-leading the creation of a campaign with marketing. And again, you can do this if the ERG leaders are comfortable with the goals and are receiving compensation.
- Finally, create an advisory board of ERG leaders, which every ERG leader sits on. Ensure this includes white men from Men as Allies, as we discussed previously. Have this advisory board meet with the C-Suite once a quarter to engage in dialogue and conversation, and raise any issues, concerns, or ideas they may have. By creating an advisory board, you prevent ERGs from becoming siloed. And you create an opportunity for the ERG leaders to create a meaningful and powerful relationship with the C-Suite where they feel recognized, seen, and heard—and become internal and external ambassadors for the company.

11

Our Ad Wasn't Racist. It Was Simply a Mistake.

In 2016, Sprint shared a short video spot where they went after competitor T-Mobile. Former Sprint CEO Marcelo Claure is seen sitting with a group of customers, discussing other phone carriers. He asks the following question: "T-Mobile. When I say 'T-Mobile' to you, just a couple of words?"[1]

A white woman sitting next to Claure exclaims, "Oh my God, the first word that came to my mind was . . . 'ghetto'!"

The mostly white crowd laughs. We see a Black man with his back to the camera bowing his head. Claure nods in agreement, and quietly says. "Yes." The white woman continues.

"I don't know . . . People who have T-Mobile are just, like . . . Why do you have T-Mobile?"

Claure then tweeted a link to the ad, which included the campaign slogan "Real Questions. Honest Answers."[2] He stated that customers featured weren't actors. "Honest answers from real people on my #ListeningTour across the country. Sometimes the truth hurts, @TMobile."

The backlash in social media was swift. Consumers pointed out that a mostly group of white individuals sat around laughing at the idea that T-Mobile was a ghetto, and that T-Mobile was associated with individuals from historically marginalized communities and cash-strapped customers. But other brands, like Sprint, were the more legitimate options.

Even as the comments came rushing in from customers on how racist the ad was, Claure didn't back down. He tweeted again in response, this time hiding behind the customers featured in the video on the use of the word ghetto: "We're sharing real comments from real customers. Maybe not the best choice of words by the customer. Not meant to offend anyone."

Sprint finally pulled the video. Claude tweeted the following apology: "My job is to listen to consumers. Our point was to share customer views. Bad judgment on our part. Apologies. Taking the video down."[3] As we will discuss later on, more in depth, many were quick to label this a non-apology.

Whether it's Sprint or another brand, we can scroll through our social feeds on any given day and see consumers sharing their outrage. Expressing disgust, anger, and shock as to how a particular brand could hurt and harm a community. And many bewildered at how that particular ad even made it to the marketplace with no one stopping it.

Here are just a few examples of other brands:

> "Hey @KelloggsUS why is the only brown corn pop on the whole cereal box the janitor? This is teaching kids racism. Yes it's a tiny thing, but when you see your kid staring at this over breakfast and realize millions of other kids are doing the same. . ." Saladin Ahmed, novelist, responding to Kellogg's Corn Pop Cereal Box, 2017.[4]

"What does America tell Black people? That we are judged by the color of our skin and that includes what is considered beautiful in this country. The tone deafness in these companies makes no sense." Consumer response to Dove Ad, 2017, where a Black woman turns into a white woman after using the body wash.[5]

"Maybe dont (sic) put gay pride and #Strangewich in the same tweet??? We're not strange."

"It's both an incredibly poor idea, for the audience, and a perfect metaphor, by some critical readings of what Pride has become." Consumer response to Hellmann's Ad, 2017.[6]

"#Dior is using a Native American dancing in traditional regalia to promote their "Sauvage" cologne. It's 2019. We must ask ourselves. Why are there still so many ads using Anti-Native Slurs and exploiting Native Americans?" Consumer response to Dior Ad, 2019.[7]

"And then H&M UK got the bright idea to feature a black boy model with 'Coolest Monkey in the Jungle' hoodie on its website. How on earth can this be? SHAME ON YOU!" Consumer response to H&M Ad, 2018.[8]

"In that Inspire Change commercial, the NFL forgot to show the part where they blackballed Colin Kaepernick, have only 3 black NFL head coaches and no majority black ownership." Consumer response to NFL ad, 2021.[9]

"The use of cartoonish serapes and sombreros as props and disguises, the misidentification of Mexican food with the stuff sold in Taco Bell, the borrowing of beloved dishes like tres leches to make versions that have little recognizability to Mexicans, this is something that we see every Cinco de Mayo and every Hispanic

Heritage Month." Professor Ignacio M. Sánchez Prado's response to "Mexican-themed" *Great British Bake Off* Episode, 2022.[10]

Despite the backlash from consumers, time and time again, I have watched leaders continue to tightly hold on to this myth: Our ad wasn't racist, it was simply a mistake. Leaders running around aghast that a brand they have worked so hard on could be called racist. Because "racist" can be too difficult a word to accept.

"How could they call us racists? We have done more for the Black community than most brands."

"I am not a racist. None of the marketers who worked on this campaign are racists. They just didn't understand the point of the video."

"I mean, the ad features a Hispanic model. How can we be racist?"

"Everyone is just so sensitive these days."

"They just throw the word racist out there to cancel us. Well, they will have to try harder than that."

Over the years, I have watched many leaders unable to come to grips with and accept the alternative: that their actions were, in fact, racist. They stay in a state of denial. Even though the racist ad goes viral, they don't inform employees of what has transpired; they let them find out in the headlines. They don't want to speak to the media; they refuse interviews. They ultimately feel forced to apologize with a vague "we are sorry for what happened" apology. They put off talking to influencers, vendors, celebrities, customers, board members, and other key stakeholders in hopes that, as one senior leader once told me, "This will all just blow over."

Because, fundamentally, many leaders don't believe what their consumers are shouting from the rooftops: this ad was racist. And as we discussed before, it didn't matter what the intent was. It didn't matter that the intent of the ad was misunderstood or misinterpreted. Because there is no time to explain intent in our digital world, and frankly, no one cares. What they do care about is impact. And the impact often is clear to just about everyone except the key decision-makers and the company power players. In many of these cases, it is a majority all-white team creating content causing harm to a histori-cally marginalized community.

What lessons can leaders learn from this type of diversity, equity, and inclusion crisis? Here are six things you need to know to navigate and survive what has happened while also avoiding repeating the same mistakes.

Accept What You Have Done

First, you must accept what has happened and what you have done. If you can't accept what the marketplace is telling you—that this piece of content is sexist, racist, homophobic, and has caused harm to a certain community—you can't move forward as a leader, as a team, or as an organization. In the end, the denial can cause more harm and can hold you back from moving forward quickly. Part of accepting what you have done is coming forward with a sincere, genuine, and authentic apology. (We will discuss apologies in more detail in the next section.)

Immediately Reach Out to Your Employees

As we said before, your employees are your forgotten consumers. Treat them as one of your most important stakeholders. Your employ-ees will either become your most loyal advocates, defending their employment experience in social media channels, explaining their own hurt and pain, and also apologizing for what has transpired. And when there is trust and commitment between employer and employee, employees will do this on their own without you asking them to. Or they will become your adversaries, setting little fires within your organization, creating an internal mutiny, and sharing their anger and disappointment with the world before you have had a chance to speak.

Let your employees know what's happening and apologize to them as well. You can send a companywide announcement, and you can equip leaders with key talking points to connect directly with their teams. You can also host employee forums to allow employees to share their concerns and questions. Reach out to specific ERGs who have been harmed by your actions. Some will want to be involved in the next steps. Others will be healing and won't want to be involved. Respect their wishes and keep them apprised on your journey of what happens next.

Then Treat This as a Crisis

When working on one particular crisis, I remember an internal corporate communications meeting where leaders said to me: "In times of crisis, it's best not to do or say anything. All of this stuff blows over. People move on to the next thing. So we do nothing."

At the time, this was contrary to the advice a communications firm had given. They advised the team to get ahead of the story; apologize, own the harm we had caused, and come up with a five-point plan on what we would do differently. Leadership refused.

Unfortunately, too many leaders continue to operate with this outdated mindset that no longer serves their company well: ignore the problem and it will just go away. In this digital age, consumers have a larger microphone than ever before. The stakes are high for brands to take a stand when injustice occurs. And when you don't, consumers are there to remind you every minute of every day that you have yet to do the right thing. According to a 2022 Trust Barometer Special Report from Edelman, 59 percent of consumers say if they don't trust the company behind the brand, they will stop buying.[11] Don't wait for the social media storm to erupt before treating this as a crisis. Part of treating it as a crisis means you put together a plan on how you will do better and be better (we will discuss that more in the next section).

Educate Yourself on Why This Was Racist

There is a difference between nodding your head and accepting that an ad is racist and actually understanding why it's racist. Ensure you and your teams discuss the details of why this piece of content was harmful. Please don't ask your Black employees or any ERGs to host discussions to explain to everyone else why this was racist. The brand team responsible for this content should do the work and educate others. If they are not capable of doing this, they need to work with their DEI team or hire a consultant to help.

Marketers focus on surprising and delighting consumers with a product or service they never expected. They do this by claiming to have studied and observed their consumer. But do they truly understand their consumer's lived experience and the history of the communities they belong to? Part of our education is understanding how racism shows up in all the media we consume. At the end of this chapter, you will find a resource guide to help educate you on understanding how racism shows up in content.

Watch Out For Diversity Propping And Diversity Dressing

In the United States alone, the Black community has $1.6 trillion in spending power.[12] According to another study, the multicultural buying power is now more than $5 trillion, which includes Black, Hispanic, Asian, Pacific Islander, Native, Indigenous, and multi-racial and multi-ethnic communities.[13] Inclusion is a driver of the business, and those brands that continue to ignore these communities will be left behind. For many, the pressure is on to find growth, and they will be tempted to check the box without doing the work on "how to sell" to a community. Remember this important insight: "nothing for us, without us." If you are trying to serve a community with authenticity and purpose, you need as many voices from that community as possible around the table. Watch out for these two diversity pitfalls.

What Is Diversity Propping?

A few years into my marketing career, I was invited to a meeting for a brand I didn't work on. I was only invited to attend without being given any details. I walked into a large room of about 15 marketers and agency colleagues. I scanned the room and immediately felt a pit in my stomach. It was clear why I had been invited: I was the only person of color in the room where they were discussing a beauty product targeted to women of color.

This is called diversity propping: using an individual from a historically marginalized community as your proof point that you have covered all bases and have the right voices at the table. When brands engage in diversity propping, they fall into the trap that one marketer, one influencer, one spokesperson represents the voice of an entire community. The burden also falls on this one individual to be the anti-racist or anti-sexist check. Finally, this individual can feel tokenized, that they were only asked to be involved because they check a box, and not for their talents and expertise.

Next time you want to invite a colleague of color to join a project, avoid diversity propping by letting them know you value their talent, expertise, and the views they bring with their life experience. Let them know you are focusing on diversity of representation; don't surprise them or tokenize them. And if they decline to join, respect their wishes.

What Is Diversity Dressing?

Recently, I saw a beauty brand post a beautiful image of a dark-skinned Black woman on their Instagram feed. A close-up image zoomed in on her facial features. And when I went to research their products online, they didn't offer an inclusive range of products—no foundations, no blushes, and no eyeshadows for darker skin tones.

This is called diversity dressing: showcasing, presenting, and amplifying "diversity of representation" when your products or services aren't inclusive. In this case, the beauty brand was checking the box toward their DEI efforts by showcasing a dark-skinned Black woman, yet their beauty products wouldn't meet her needs.

Diversity dressing can also go beyond trying to pretend to address racial inequities. Vogue Business called out fashion brands that were including plus-size or curve models on runways and in campaigns.[14,15] Yet, increased representation in campaigns and on runways hasn't translated to inclusive sizing in stores and on racks. This is another important reminder that you have to do the work to make sure products and services are inclusive to avoid diversity dressing.

Finally, Listen to the Whispers, They Are the Loudest

When I was working on one particular DEI crisis where a brand was accused of creating racist content, a junior marketer expressed concern with the campaign and voicing his concern with the ad before it was launched. He said it made him uncomfortable but didn't quite have the language to express what he felt was wrong. The head of market research silenced him, saying that it had been thoroughly vetted and tested by consumers. There was no need to raise any concerns because there was nothing to be concerned about.

Don't discount the junior people on your team. Listen closely to the whispers and the quiet voices, the ones who are hesitant to share what they really think but find the courage to do so. Those words should carry weight and should be the loudest. They can be the catalyst for unlocking conversations on your team and stop you from putting out content that will hurt your consumer.

Finally, we know it's important to discuss the ways in which companies and brands create harm. It's also equally important to acknowledge all the brands that are growing and learning on their journey to be an ally and authentically serving Black communities. Dove co-founding the CROWN Coalition Act[16] to fight hair discrimination; Adidas partnering with Soul Cap for inclusive-sized swim caps;[17] Ben and Jerry's on a mission to dismantle white supremacy;[18] Sephora fighting racial bias in retail and co-founding Open to All pledge;[19] Target, Disney, and Old Navy embracing and lifting up Black Santa Claus;[20] Good Humor taking on the racist ice cream truck song;[21] and Procter and Gamble's films "The Look," about racial bias Black men face, and "The Talk,"[22] about parents talking to their children about racial bias, to name just a few. These brands remind us that when it comes to the work of inclusion, there are no shortcuts or quick fixes. And many of these brands will make mistakes and can't let that one moment deter them from continuing their journey to be more inclusive. We, the leaders behind the brands and the companies, have to commit to doing the work of inclusion for the long term.

Understanding Why Consumers Call Out Content and Products for Being Racist

The following examples provide a baseline education and understanding for marketers and business leaders of how content and products in the marketplace draw from the institution of slavery, which lasted for centuries. They show us that the institution of slavery, as well as the segregation that followed, continues to have modern day repercussions. Many of these have been engrained deeply into our subconscious and psyche. On my journey to be an ally to the Black community, here are just some of the resources I use to continue to educate myself on the origins of racist content: National Museum of African American History & Culture;[23] Black History & Culture

Academy, founded by Elizabeth Leiba;[24] Jim Crow Museum at Ferris State University and the work of Dr. David Pilgrim;[25] and African American History: From Emancipation to Present (2010) as part of Open Yale Course, taught by Dr. Jonathan Holloway.[26]

My intent in sharing the following examples is not to cause further harm to the Black community. My hope is that by sharing these marketplace examples, we collectively will not allow history to repeat itself. And the impact will be that we will not continue to deny that ads can, in fact, be racist. Finally, the consumers we look to serve will genuinely trust and believe the positive impact we are trying to make.

1. *"Romanticizing Slavery"*

Romanticizing the institution of slavery and not reflecting the reality when many enslaved Black women were raped and abused by white enslavers. It also represents the white man as a savior and ignores the fact that so many enslaved people escaped on their own.[27]

Marketplace example: Ancestry.com's film (2019) "Inseparable" shows a Black woman and a white man who are in love attempting to escape what appears to be the Civil War-era South.[28] It depicts a white man holding up a ring and telling a Black woman wearing Civil War-era clothing that they can be together if they escape to the North. The woman says nothing as the scene fades to black, with the line: "Without you, the story stops here." The ad was taken down after public backlash and accusation of whitewashing slavery. With that ad, Ancestry's intent was to be part of its effort to tell "important stories from history." Ancestry pulled the ad and issued an apology.

2. *"Popularizing Shackles"*

Commercializing and making popular the use of shackles, which physically restrained, dehumanized, and degraded Black people for centuries. "The shackles were used to transport captured Africans to slavery in the Americas, part of the "Middle Passage" of the transatlantic slave trade."[29]

Marketplace example: Adidas "shackle shoes" were cancelled after launching in 2012. Their apology: "The design of the JS Roundhouse Mid is nothing more than the designer Jeremy Scott's outrageous and unique take on fashion and has nothing to do with slavery. We apologize if people are offended by the design and we are withdrawing our plans to make them available in the marketplace."[30]

3. "Propagating Blackface"

The portrayal of Blackface is when people darken their skin. Centuries ago, white actors would do comedic performances of "blackness" in what was known as minstrel shows. White actors dressed in exaggerated costumes would use shoe polish, paint, or burnt cork to paint on enlarged lips and other exaggerated features.[31]

Blackface is steeped in centuries of racism. It peaked in popularity during an era when recently emancipated enslaved Black individuals demanded civil rights. Blackface used in minstrel shows was a way to stereotype Black people as lazy, ignorant, and prone to thievery and a way to continue to dehumanize them. It was used as a tool to authenticate whiteness.

Marketplace examples:

In 2019, Gucci was selling a black turtleneck sweater that pulled up over the bottom half of the face with a cut out and oversized red lips around the mouth.[32] Social media users said it resembled Blackface, and this backlash also unfolded in February during Black History Month. The Gucci designer apologized in a statement and said his design was actually inspired by the late Leigh Bowery, a performance artist, club promoter, and fashion designer who often used flamboyant face makeup and costumes.

The Katy Perry Shoe Collection launched an Ora Face Block Heel and Rue Face Slip-On Loafers in summer 2018 as part of a collection in nine colors, including black. Both styles include the same nose, protruding eyes, and full red lips. Consumers immediately took to social channels and drew comparisons to Blackface. The shoes were removed from the Katy Perry Collections with an apology.[33]

In 2020, outerwear label Moncler created a collection including a cartoonish figure called "Malfi" featured on its jackets and shirts. Consumers were outraged that "Malfi" resembled Blackface figures from minstrel shows. The brand apologized.[34]

4. "Dehumanizing Black People with Use of Monkeys"

Dehumanizing of Black people was used as a vehicle to justify the institution of slavery for centuries. Robert Guillaume, in the documentary *Story of a People* (1993), explains:

> "To justify slavery, black Americans had to be dehumanized. A moral and legal framework to support slavery was constructed at the same time. The distortion of the black image begins here. If it is believed that a man is inferior, subhuman, it becomes easy to treat him as a pet, a toy, an object of comic relief, a crazed lower animal who must be controlled and ruled."[35]

Marketplace examples:

Prada's Otto Keychain in 2018 was a monkey figurine called Otto depicted as a black animal with overly large red lips. Consumers quickly pointed out the product as being racist. The brand issued an apology and removed the products.[36]

In 2020, the company overseeing Dr. Seuss children's books announced it would stop publishing six books due to racist imagery.[37] In *If I Ran the Zoo*, Dr. Seuss depicted African characters as monkeys, and several other books also included racist imagery.[38]

5. *"Reinforcing the Myth of the Mammy"*

The Mammy caricature was used to justify economic discrimination and racism during the Jim Crow era, reinforcing the stereotype that Black women were only capable of being domestic workers. During slavery, the Mammy was proof that Black women were happy as enslaved people. She was portrayed as always being happy and loyal in images and in the media.[39]

Marketplace examples:

The brands Aunt Jemima and Mrs. Butterworth's represent the dark comfort some Americans may feel when it comes to black servitude: pancakes served routinely and normally at their kitchen table. The origin of Aunt Jemima's dates back to minstrel shows portraying the Mammy.[40] Mrs. Butterworth's origin is linked to the character of a maid from *Gone with the Wind*.[41] In 2020, both brands publicly acknowledged the characters were based on racial stereotypes.

In 2021, Aunt Jemima (part of PepsiCo) rebranded to The Pearl Milling Company.[42] In 2020, Conagra, the company that owns Mrs. Butterworth's, also promised to undergo a complete brand and packaging review. Consumers are waiting to see those changes.[43]

6. *"Reinforcing the Myth of Tom"*

Similar to the Mammy caricature, the Tom caricature portrayed Black men as loyal and happy servants. The Tom caricature was also born in defense of slavery, showing Black men as being content and faithful. Tom is always smiling and is positioned as the server: cook, butler, waiter, porter, or fieldworker in images and media.[44] Additionally, in the Jim Crow era, Black men were addressed as "Boy" or "Uncle" and Black women were addressed as "Girl" or "Aunty" and they were never addressed by their name.[45]

Marketplace examples:

In 2020, Mars Inc. announced it would review its brand Uncle Ben's. The use of the word "uncle" and the image of the Black man on the package "serving" was racist in origin.[46] In 2021, the brand was renamed Ben's Original.[47]

In 2020, B&G Food said it was reviewing its brand Cream of Wheat, founded in 1893. The original mascot was Rastus, a racial stereotype from minstrel shows. In the early 1900s, they replaced the image with a Black man happy to serve and smiling.[48] The company has since removed the image of the Black chef from its packaging.[49]

7. *Propagating Colorism: Lighter Is Better*

Colorism upholds and values white standards of beauty, and it is a product of racism. It continues to be pervasive, whether we're aware of it or not. The preference for lighter skin over darker skin is still prevalent in many communities, including Black, Latin, and Asian and is not discussed enough openly.

The institution of slavery created a caste system where enslaved Black people were differentiated based on their skin tones. Lighter-skinned enslaved people were many times favored by white enslavers, and often the product of rape and abuse of enslaved women. They were often forced to work inside the home, as opposed to being forced to do outdoor fieldwork and were in closer contact with their white enslavers. Once the institution of slavery ended, colorism still endured. Light skin and privilege became linked.[50]

Marketplace examples:

In 2017, Nivea was accused of colorism when their campaign in Africa "Natural Fairness Body Lotion" was pushing visibly fairer skin with their whitening products. The brand apologized.[51]

In 2018, a Heineken ad featured a bartender sliding a bottle of Heineken Light. The bottle passes several Black people before it arrives to a lighter-skinned woman. The tag line: *Sometimes lighter is better.* The brand apologized and pulled the ad.[52]

In 2019, Waitrose, a UK grocery chain, apologized regarding the naming of three chocolate ducklings after being accused of racism. The "Waitrose Trio of Chocolate Easter Ducklings" contained white, milk, and dark chocolate versions, which were named "Fluffy," "Crispy" and "Ugly," respectively. Consumers questioned why the darkest duckling was labeled the "Ugly" duckling.[53]

8. Using Language Tied to Slavery and Segregation

Daniel Decatur Emmett composed "Dixie" in 1859. It was a minstrel song that included the famous lyrics "Away, away, away, down south in the Dixie." The song became the national anthem for the Confederacy during the Civil War. "Dixie" became a nickname for the Southern states. Additionally, "Dixie" is tied back to the Mason-Dixon Line, a boundary between Maryland and Pennsylvania that was drawn in 1767. It later become an informal delineation between the Southern states and the states to the north.[54]

Marketplace example:

> In 2020, The Dixie Chicks, an American country music band, changed their name to The Chicks. They announced the change on their website, stating: "We want to meet this moment."[55]

In American history, the Antebellum period is thought of as the period before the Civil War. "Antebellum" in advertising has come to be associated with romanticizing this period, memories of grand plantation-style architecture and huge landscapes and women in ornate dresses. The fashion and architecture of this time were built off the institution of slavery. Antebellum romanticizes a painful part of our history and the enslavement of Black people.[56]

Marketplace example:

In 2020, The country-rock act Lady Antebellum changed its name to Lady A. The band said on its website: "Our hearts have been stirred with conviction, our eyes opened wide to the injustices, inequality and biases black women and men have always faced and continue to face every day. Blind spots we didn't even know existed have been revealed."[57] The band originally named themselves after taking a photograph outside an Antebellum home in Nashville. Lady A was then sued by Anita White, who also went by the name Lady A since the 1980s and accused the band of trying to erase her. The band settled the lawsuit with the Black blues singer.[58]

9. Misrepresenting Black Families

Black families are continuously misrepresented and stereotyped. We see language used to describe Black families like "broken families" and "working/working class families."[59] One harmful myth that continues to be perpetuated: Black fathers are absent from their families. A Center for Disease Control study showed that Black fathers have "Proven to be just as involved with their children as other dads in similar living conditions—or more so."[60]

Marketplace example:

In 2020, Burt's Bees posted an ad with families in their holiday pajamas. All of the white families featured included a mom and dad. The only Black family featured showed a Black mother and her children. They apologized for perpetuating stereotypes of Black families.[61] (They didn't acknowledge that they also didn't include a family with two moms or two dads.)

In 2018, Target apologized and pulled a greeting card they were selling in store: a card with an image of a Black couple with the words "Baby Daddy."[62] The term can be considered derogatory, describing an absent father of a single woman's child. As stated in the Color of Change Report, *Changing the Narrative about Black Families*, "What's the difference between having 'blended families' and 'baby mamas' and 'baby daddies'? Typically it's the race of the family members. These terms have a context-specific meaning within Black culture. But when used by people who are not Black . . . they have the effects of undermining the seriousness of a relationship or implying the lack of a personal responsibility and are especially aimed at women."[63]

Tips for Focusing on Creating Inclusive Content and Products

Here are some tips for focusing on creating inclusive content and products. Start by asking yourself the following questions:

Who is sitting around the table and why?

We know that diversity of thought doesn't happen without diversity of representation. When you are at the start of developing a product concept, a story board, or brainstorming for a campaign idea, please pause and look around. Who is sitting around the table and why? Do you have representation from different communities, different disciplines, and different functions? Ensure you have the right voices around the table: this includes your marketing team and agencies and partners you work with. Be as inclusive and intentional at the start of any innovation process.

What voices are you including in your ecosystem?

As we have discussed, you should have focused efforts to hire, develop, and promote more talent on your teams with a focus on diversity of representation. Go one step further and ensure the ecosystem of partners is not overlooked. Your job as the client is to provide timely and candid feedback to partners, particularly if your agencies don't have talent from historically marginalized communities staffed on projects. As the client, hold agencies accountable during the review process and ask for continued updates on their diversity, equity, and inclusion plans. Expand your supplier diversity efforts and be specific on broadening your list of agencies and marketing consultants. Remember that including only one singular voice at the table places the burden on that one individual and also tokenizes them. As we discussed before, do the work as a leader to ensure multiple voices have not just a seat at the table, but also that they are seen, valued, and heard, ensuring them that their contributions matter.

Why do we focus on featuring racially ambiguous models?

Let's stop focusing on racially ambiguous models. Remove this language from all briefs and marketing materials. Start featuring dark-skinned models, honoring and celebrating them, and use this as an opportunity to shatter stereotypes in advertising and perpetuating white beauty standards.

Who is in front of the camera and who is behind the camera?

Set targets for who is in front of the camera. How many models from historically marginalized communities do you cast? Are you measuring your influencer base and who you are featuring? Who are you shining a spotlight on and why? Finally, who is behind the camera? Do you also have diverse slates when it

(continued)

comes to selecting directors and production companies? Start measuring both who gets to be behind and in front of the camera.

How can you create an inclusive set experience?

Ensuring you have a diversity of representation is one thing. Ensuring you have created an inclusive set experience is another. Have your make-up artists and hair stylists only ever worked with white talent? Do they have the right shades of foundation, blush, and lipstick? Why are you asking talent to straighten their hair? Create a list of on-set reminders and appoint someone to be the set ambassador who can ensure the cast feels welcome and stop any biased language in its tracks: *It's hard to contour and highlight a large, wide nose. Why is your hair so difficult to work with? And your dark skin doesn't really work with this top.*

How can you ensure inclusivity in products and services?

Ensure you have inclusivity in the products and services you offer in the marketplace.

For example, if you are a beauty brand, you need to ensure products beyond just the foundation work on darker skin tones. If you are a coaching platform selling personalized coaching services, ensure you have representation of coaches from historically marginalized communities. If you are co-creating your spring collection with fashion influencers, ensure you have a diversity of representation of designers as collaborators. Review the products and services you already have in the marketplace, as well as the concepts in your innovation pipeline. Create and rally around a plan for the needed additions, changes, and revisions. When it comes to serving any community authentically, nothing for us, without us. You can't sell to a community if you don't have an understanding of their needs.

MYTH

12 | We Aren't Apologizing. People Need to Stop Being So Sensitive.

"So I said him, instead of her. Got it," a leader snapped back. "It's not a big deal."

This was the response I received from this leader after I approached about something a colleague shared with me regarding a meeting that took place earlier in the week. This leader and another colleague repeatedly misgendered another person in the meeting even though others tried to correct them in the moment. Apparently this was not the first time this occurred.

"Well, both of you in the meeting used the wrong pronouns repeatedly, and this isn't the first time," I countered, wanting him to understand the harm they had caused. "It was you and . . ."

"Ok, ok, so maybe we both did. I mean ok, so he's now a she? It's none of my business," he shrugged his shoulders. "We need to focus on a strong close to the year."

"I know an apology would mean a lot to her. You can . . ."

"We aren't apologizing," he exclaimed, a bit flustered and taken aback by my recommendation. "People need to stop being so sensitive."

We sat in silence for a few moments. I started to get up and leave the conference room.

"Wait," he said. I stopped. I thought maybe he had a change of heart.

"How about you just apologize for us?"

In my work with leaders and companies, coaching someone to apologize can be an extraordinarily difficult task. Why is it so difficult to apologize? What holds us back? Why can't we just apologize and move forward?

As we discussed earlier in the example of the racist ad, the biggest barrier we face with apologizing is this: If you don't believe or can't accept that you have done something wrong, that you have harmed someone else, you will never want to truly apologize for your actions. Providing an apology won't be something you think of doing.

In addition to brands and companies causing harm, individuals knowingly or unknowingly cause harm every day in our workplaces:

"Oh, I wasn't supposed to pet her seeing dog? What do you call it? A support animal? Well, I didn't know, so an apology wouldn't make sense because I didn't know."

"Okay, so her name isn't Shilpa, it's Mita. I know they are the only two South Asian women in the marketing department. It's too bad they feel that way, but I don't feel the need to apologize because I do this all the time. You just need to tell them I am not very good with names."

"Yup, I came as a Mexican man to the office party. I wore a colorful poncho, a big sombrero hat, and a long black mustache.

Trust me, no one was offended. It would be ridiculous to apologize for a Halloween costume."

"One day Christina wears her hair very short, and the next day it's in very long braids, and then it's just really big. So, yes, right before she presented, I asked how she finds the time to constantly change her hair. Honestly, it's distracting and unprofessional. So I am unclear as to why you are asking me to apologize."

"Sure, I did ask him about his wife a few times. I didn't know he had a husband. Well . . . maybe he had told me that before but I can't remember. What's the big deal? Can't you just apologize for me?"

Here are some of the things that hold us back from apologizing:

- We don't believe we did anything wrong.
- We don't want to be perceived as being weak.
- We don't really care about the other person.
- We don't want to feel bad about ourselves.
- We don't believe an apology will do any good.

What Does it Mean to Misgender Someone?

Misgendering happens when you intentionally or unintentionally refer to an individual in a way that doesn't align with their affirmed gender. In the example I shared, on more than one occasion, the leader referred to a colleague as "he" and not "she." Getting pronouns incorrect is one example of misgendering.

For our transgender and nonbinary colleagues, this experience of being misgendered over and over can be demoralizing. Imagine this happening to you daily and the emotional and physical toll it would have: of not feeling seen or valued and
(continued)

(*continued*)

wondering whether or not you should correct someone or just let it go. Take the time to learn and honor a person's pronouns. When in doubt, just ask. If you get it wrong, apologize and say you will use the correct pronouns in the future. And make sure you do so. If you have repeatedly misgendered someone, we will review in this next section how you can choose to genuinely apologize.

And when we believe the myth that *we shouldn't apologize and that people should stop being so sensitive,* we don't recognize the further harm we will cause. In my time coaching leaders, here are the three questions I ask individuals to keep in mind when it comes to apologizing:

1. Why Should I Apologize?

In our journey to be more inclusive leaders, we must embrace humility when we have made mistakes, when we have caused harm, and when we have hurt someone. So why should you apologize?

Because when you apologize, you:

- Open communication again if you haven't been in contact/ avoiding each other.
- Accept and acknowledge that you were wrong.
- Express regret for what you did.
- Take accountability for your actions.
- Recognize what you did wrong and learn from your mistakes.
- Take the first step in rebuilding trust and repair in the relationship.

Not apologizing can also further damage your work and personal relationships. It can lead to resentment, anger, and more misunderstandings in the future. As we discussed earlier, intent and impact both matter. If I cause a colleague harm and never apologize, that individual may assume I have negative intent no matter what I do or say in the future. And remember, even if I decide to apologize, the person who I harmed might not be willing to accept the apology in the moment. They may never accept the apology. And that's their right. Just because we apologize doesn't mean we assume that they accept the apology and are willing to move forward.

2. How Should I Apologize?

How you apologize matters. The context and circumstances also matter. When we get to discussing how brands and companies choose to apologize, it will most likely be in written form. Apologizing in a timely manner makes a difference. It's best not to wait to apologize. And it's never too late to apologize to a colleague for something you did wrong.

When apologizing to another person, it should be a one-on-one interaction, unless there are several individuals you caused harm to. How you apologize also depends on how well you know the person(s) and the best way in which you think they might be able to receive the apology. Consider the following options:

- Face-to-face, either in person or over video.
- Written form, either an email, text, or a handwritten note, with a follow-up conversation.
- Over the phone, where you pick up the phone and call and potentially leave a message if they don't answer.

A person who has been harmed by your actions may not want to meet or talk to you live. They may still be healing from the hurt and harm that you inflicted. In this case, you can still write them an apology. That way they can receive your apology on their own terms when they are ready. Remember, just because you are ready to apologize doesn't mean they are ready to receive it or even forgive you.

3. What Should I Say When Apologizing?

What you say when you apologize will set the tone for whether it's sincere, genuine, and heartfelt. And whether the person you are apologizing to believes you and accepts the apology. They may also choose to forgive you when you apologize, at a future date, or they may never forgive you at all. All you can control is how you apologize and what you do after you apologize.

We have all received the "non-apology" or the fake apology. It's when the person who has caused you harm or offense won't actually take accountability or acknowledge why they are apologizing in the first place. It is usually something along the lines:

- I am sorry you feel that way.
- I was only joking.
- Mita told me to apologize, so I am sorry.
- You know I didn't mean that.
- I am sorry that you misunderstood what I meant to say.
- I probably shouldn't have done or said that.
- I am sorry if you feel that I did something wrong.
- I am sorry, but maybe you are being too sensitive.
- I apologize if you think I offended you.

When I apologize to a colleague, I follow this simple formula:

- First, say that you are sorry. Full stop. Just apologize.
- Second, be specific on what you did. This can be a one-time act or something that has happened on more than one occasion.
- Third, commit to doing better.

Here are some apology examples:

- I am sorry. I know that your preferred pronouns are she/her/
  hers. I should never have repeatedly used incorrect pronouns. I
  am going to continue to reflect and educate myself on the
  painful impact misgendering someone can have.
- I apologize. I know your name is Mita, and not Shilpa. And I
  have repeatedly called you Shilpa. I know I have hurt you and
  embarrassed you. I am sorry. I am going to continue to think
  about how I can show up as a better ally for you and educate
  myself on the importance of names.
- I am sorry. My Halloween costume was stereotyping and making fun of Mexican men. It was not funny; I now know it was
  hurtful and harmful. If there's anyone else you know in the
  office who was hurt by my costume, I would like to personally
  apologize to them as well.

After you have caused harm and then provide a sincere and genuine apology, now begins the work to do better, and be better. It can
be a long road to rebuild trust with those individuals who have been
hurt and harmed by your actions, depending on the context and circumstances. When apologizing, ask at the end if there is anything you
can do for the other person now, or any other support they may need
for you. They may decline or may ask you to do something.

All you can do is show, with your actions and your words going
forward, that you have learned from the harmed you caused. And that
in your case, history will not repeat itself, and you may help others
not repeat the mistakes and harm you have caused.

Finally, you have to be ready to apologize. No one can force you
or convince you to do it. Because when it is forced, it can cause more
damage. And you should never put anyone in a position to apologize
on your behalf. Our journey to be more inclusive leaders starts with

owning and delivering our own apologies. This goes for individual apologies as well as how we lead our teams through apologies that must be delivered by brands and companies.

How to Help Your Company Apologize

As discussed in the previous section, on any given day, it seems like companies are being accused of racist, sexist, homophobic, or non-inclusive content, products, or experiences. These so-called mistakes are hurtful and damaging to a number of communities. Consumers take to their social media channels to unleash their anger, their outrage, and their proclamations of "I am never buying this again!" According to the annual Edelman Trust Barometer, approximately 60 percent of consumers buy from brands based on their values and beliefs.[1] The belief-driven buyer is here to stay: They will walk away from products and services that have lost their trust.

So as leaders, we can no longer avoid the inevitable. It's not if, but when, they will have to deal with a content or product-related crisis negatively impacting and causing further harm to historically marginalized communities. And just like in any relationship, how you apologize matters.

Apologies must be timely, heartfelt, and must acknowledge the wrongdoing and prove that the individual who has caused offense wants to do better and be better. Here are three things companies must do when apologizing to regain trust and loyalty from consumers and the greater marketplace:

Be Timely

In the world of social media, you must swiftly address consumers within 24 to 48 hours. Don't bury what happened; don't delete the tweet or pretend that the offense didn't occur. Don't wait for dozens of influencers and key media outlets to pick up on what happened before you address the issue at hand. The apology carries more weight when it's addressed quickly and proactively; silence can speak volumes and create more anger and distress. Whatever you share externally should first be shared internally. Remember, your employees are your forgotten consumer; don't forget about apologizing to them as well.

If you are anxious or concerned about how to apologize, hire the right help and support. And make sure you listen to their advice and perspective. Unlike a personal, one-to-one apology, remember that this apology will most likely be read and shared by many, many people. The speed of the apology and the actual content of the apology are both equally important.

When Lizzo, an artist and outspoken social and political activist, released the song "Grrrls" from her album *Special*, it was surprising she would choose to include the word "spaz." The word is a well-known slur against individuals with disabilities. There was significant criticism on social media from individuals with disabilities and allies of the community. Lizzo apologized publicly in less than 48 hours.[2] She committed to changing the song lyrics, sharing her personal apology on Instagram. Many of her fans and advocates for individuals with disabilities who were the first to publicly criticize her applauded and accepted her heartfelt apology. Lizzo didn't hesitate in admitting the harm she had caused.

Be Specific

"We are sorry we missed the mark" or "we are sorry we offended you" or "we heard feedback you are upset so we are sorry" doesn't cut it anymore. Be specific on what you did wrong to educate others from repeating your mistake. Given that many are reading this public apology, including leaders at other companies, it's a moment to share what you have learned. For example, this is an opportunity to clearly be specific on why an ad was racist so others don't just say, yes, that ad was racist. But they understand specifically why it caused hurt and harm. And if you decide not to be specific and explain the gravity of the mistake that was made, you will likely be called out by consumers for issuing a "non-apology."

In contrast to the non-apology, Lizzo's apology was specific and vulnerable: "It's been brought to my attention that there is a harmful word in my new song 'GRRRLS'. Let me make one thing clear: I never want to promote derogatory language. As a fat black woman in America, I've had many hurtful words used against me so I understand the power words can have (whether intentionally or in my case, unintentionally)."

Be Prepared to Rebuild Trust, and Build It Again

Remember, the apology is important—and what happens next is even more important. In a personal one-to-one apology, the other individual is watching for signs and actions to see how you will invest in repairing the relationship. In a public apology, there will be many more individuals watching and waiting to see what your company does next. As leaders, you must make a long-term commitment to rebuild trust with the communities who may have walked away. The diversity, equity, and inclusion crisis you find yourself in could become a real opportunity to show up as an industry leader and make an impact in the greater ecosystem. But more important, it's an opportunity to show up in a meaningful way to those who have been harmed and let them know by your actions that you are on a journey to do better and be better.

As we conclude this section, we leave you with some examples of brands and companies who provided apologies and continue to be on a journey to rebuild trust with their consumers. These examples serve as a reminder that we can cause harm, make progress, cause harm again, and make progress.

Starbucks   Former Starbucks CEO Kevin Johnson's apology was a best-in-class example of how companies can get apologies right. Johnson acknowledged the harm when, in 2018, two Black men in a Philadelphia Starbucks store were wrongfully arrested while having a business meeting. As the CEO, he took the lead to apologize on behalf of the company, and it was timely and detailed. Johnson said he hoped to meet with the two men personally to apologize, planned to meet with law enforcement and the local community, and specifically said that "Starbucks stands firmly against discrimination or racial profiling."[3]

In 2020, Starbucks then when on to announce that it would tie executives' compensation to creating a more diverse workforce with specific goals. By 2025, Starbucks aspires to have 30 percent of its corporate employees and 40 percent retail and manufacturing employees identify as Black, indigenous, or as people of color.[4] Starbucks has also publicly shared the demographic makeup of its workforce.[5]

H&M   In our last section, we reviewed retailer H&M's racist ad incident, which occurred in 2018. H&M apologized for an ad featuring a Black child who was wearing a hoodie with the phrase "coolest monkey in the jungle." Their apology, which could have been more genuine and specific, was as follows: "We sincerely apologize for offending people with this image of a printed hooded top. The image has been removed from all online channels and the product will not be for sale in the United States. We believe in diversity and inclusion in all that we do and will be reviewing all our internal policies accordingly to avoid any future issues."[6]

While their apology may have been lackluster, a year later, H&M decided to invite a reporter from The Refinery 29 to discuss with the retailer directly what had happened. In "The Real Story Behind H&M's Racist Monkey Sweatshirt," by Connie Wang, we get a glimpse into what the company had been grappling with since the racist ad went viral: how did this happen? As Wang says, H&M had been on a search for answers: was it their employees? Their processes? Their culture? Wang speaks to the mother of the boy who was featured in the sweatshirt ad. She spends time with Annie Wu, who had been promoted to be the new global head of diversity and inclusivity for the retailer based in Stockholm. She also attends an unconscious bias training workshop with H&M employees. She spends time with employees in various departments and at their headquarters. The retailer seems to give Wang full access as they search for answers, together.[7]

H&M inviting the media into their company to do an in-depth piece one year after the racist ad went viral showcases vulnerability and humility. It's a good example of one way to rebuild lost trust after the apology. In this case, H&M is opening up to show the journey they have been on, the progress they want to make, and reminds us that there is opportunity for other companies to reflect on where they are in their journey, a year after a crisis occurs.

Sephora   Sephora, once accused by consumers of racist in-store experiences in 2019,[8] has now become a leader in its industry when it comes to building inclusive companies. The retailer continues to do the work to rebuild trust with consumers. Sephora commissioned the first-ever racial bias in retail study[9] and co-founded the Mitigate Racial Bias in Retail Charter Pledge with the nonprofit Open to All.[10] Over 29 retail brands have signed the pledge to date, with Sephora leading the way. Sephora was the first major retailer to commit to dedicating at least 15 percent of shelf space to Black-owned brands[11] through the 15 Percent Pledge.[12] They also incubate BIPOC-founded brands in a six-month-long program to grow and support more BIPOC brands. They have also increased the amount of Spanish-language content they produce and ensured closed captioning in all their Instagram video content, in addition to other key initiatives to create a more inclusive shopping experience. Sephora also publicly shared the demographic makeup of its workforce in a detailed DEI report outlining all of its work.[13]

Sesame Street Place   In 2022, a video of an employee in a Sesame Street character costume ignoring two small Black girls during a parade at Sesame Street Place Philadelphia went viral. The two Black girls have their hands out for a hug; the Sesame Street employee walks by them and waves them off. The two girls stand there looking sad, confused, and disappointed. This same character was seen hugging other children (who mostly appeared to be white on video) along the parade.[14]

The first statement issued was not an apology, but rather an announcement that it was "a misunderstanding." It read as follows: "The performer portraying the Rosita character has confirmed that the 'no' hand gesture seen several times in the video was not directed to any specific person, rather it was a response to multiple requests from someone in the crowd who asked Rosita to hold their child for a photo which is not permitted. The Rosita performer did not intentionally ignore the girls and is devastated about the misunderstanding."[15]

As the video became viral and the media reached out to Sesame Street Place Philadelphia for further details, a day later the statement was updated to become an apology on their social media channels: "We did speak with and apologize to the family for the experience, offering a return trip for a meet and greet personalized experience with the characters." It went on to say: "No child should ever leave our park feeling disappointed or ignored. That is the opposite of what our park is intended to inspire in children. We want every child who comes to the park to have a positive, memorable experience. And we commit to learn everything we can from this situation and make needed changes. As noted previously, we will provide additional training for Sesame Place employees to help them better understand, recognize, and deliver an inclusive, equitable, and entertaining experience to our guests."[16] So, while they didn't apologize to begin with, they replaced the non-apology with an apology swiftly.

In the weeks after the incident, Sesame Street Place, owned by SeaWorld, announced a series of detailed DEI initiatives. This included a racial equity assessment that is "a review of policies, processes, and practices that impact guests, employees, suppliers, and the community to identify opportunities for improvement." Additionally, all employees will "participate in a substantive training and education program designed to address bias, promote inclusion, prevent discrimination, and ensure all guests and employees feel safe and welcome. This training will be incorporated into the onboarding of all new employees and will become a regular part of our training and workforce development."[17] Finally, all of their initiatives have been developed and are overseen by national experts in civil rights and DEI. An important move to ensure they work is being done credibly as they rebuild trust both internally and externally.

In summary, apologizing is one of the most underrated and most underutilized simple acts a leader can offer to try and start to mend relationships. On our journey to be more inclusive leaders, we will individually cause harm and make mistakes. Our teams, our brands, and our companies will all at some point find themselves at crossroads: to apologize or not to apologize, that is the question. By apologizing, we strive to become better leaders and better versions of ourselves. When we are humble and admit our mistakes, it inspires those around us to do the same. This is the real work it takes to build inclusive leaders, who in turn help to build inclusive cultures.

Tips on Apologizing When You Have Caused Harm

Here are some reminder tips on how to apologize when you as an individual have caused harm:

- Only apologize if you are truly sorry; please don't offer a non-apology.
- By not apologizing, you may create further damage to the relationship.
- Be timely about the apology.
- How you apologize depends on the context of the situation and how well you know each other.
- Never ask the person you have harmed to educate you on the harm you caused.
- Be specific on what you did and why you now understand that it was harmful.
- Don't provide an apology expecting to be forgiven.
- Understand the person you harmed may not want to hear or accept your apology.
- Never ask anyone to apologize on your behalf.
- Encourage your colleagues around you to apologize when they have caused harm.

After an apology, commit to investing in rebuilding that relationship with how you show up at work for that person in every single interaction moving forward.

13

We Can Work from Home Now. The Future of Work Is Inclusive.

> "The pandemic has changed everything. We can work from home now. The future of work is inclusive."

A leader announced this on stage as the first wave of the pandemic came to a close. He was met with applause in the room, while clap emoji hands filled the Zoom boxes on the screens. The pandemic has forever changed the way we work. We will never go back to the way things used to be. Ninety-minute commutes each way. Unable to take time off to prioritize your family. Trapped in your cubicle with your boss monitoring when you started and ended your day. Pressured to come into the office even when you were sick. Unable to persuade leaders to allow individuals to call into meetings or even use video because everyone was required to be in person.

According to McKinsey Research, in the beginning of the pandemic, 80 percent of individuals surveyed enjoyed working from home and 48 percent said that they were more productive than before.[1] They enjoyed great flexibility in managing their work and personal lives. Leaders were optimistic they could access more talent pools, with the ability to hire from anywhere in the world. They could embrace more technology to boost productivity. And they could relook at office space, reinvesting any cost savings back into the business and into their employees.

Because suddenly, "the future of work" had arrived. And for the better part of two years, many of us were relegated to working from our homes. During a time of devastating loss and grief, we re-evaluated many things, including where we worked, how we worked, and what we worked on. For many of us, we questioned why we worked and who we worked for. It was a seismic shift; it was a big win, and it transformed our workplaces. So yes, many leaders have been convinced the future of work is destined to be inclusive.

In debunking this final myth, we must recognize that "the future of work" is an important component of building inclusive cultures. Many of us are no longer relegated to be within the same four walls every single workday, in one particular building in one specific city.

This shift enables us to reimagine "the future of work." This also directly influences how we can reimagine inclusion in our organizations. However, just because "where we work from" has changed for many of us doesn't automatically mean the future of work is inclusive. As we discuss throughout the book, reimagining what inclusion looks like in our organizations will take dedicated time, effort, and commitment from each of us.

This final myth also reminds us that we can't just check the box and cling to one win we have had. Because building an inclusive culture is more than just about where we work from. Along with the ability to now work from home, I have had many a leader tout to me the important wins on their inclusion journeys:

"We have a Black board member."

"We launched a campaign authentically featuring the LBGTQ+ community this year and it won an industry award."

"We have our first ever woman CEO and she was featured in *Forbes*."

"We have increased representation of Hispanic talent by 10 percent."

"We were named the #1 company for mothers."

"We have ensured all of our video content has captions and descriptions."

"We have an internship specifically for students from historically Black colleges and universities."

Of course, these wins—the small ones and the big ones—are important moments. We should celebrate them. But be wary of getting too comfortable, patting ourselves on the back, and falling prey to simply checking the box. Because when we cling to those wins and don't let go, thinking the work is done, we may actually stop doing the work; we may stop making progress.

Consider the following wins you may accomplish in your organization:

- You exceeded your sales target this quarter.
- You found $10M of cost savings by streamlining key processes.
- You signed on your first Fortune 100 client.
- You raised your first round of funding.
- You successfully broke into an adjacent category, delivering significant growth.

Would you stop putting in the work, halt progress, and cling to that one big accomplishment, that one win? Or would you be so excited by your accomplishment that it would push you to accelerate your efforts? So why is it when it comes to building inclusive workplaces, we seem to stop when we are just getting started?

The work to build inclusive workplaces is step-by-step, and day-by-day. Each of us plays a role in ensuring we don't stop doing the work. As leaders, we cannot cling to the myth that simply because we all can work from home now, our solution to creating a more inclusive culture has arrived. One win won't be the only thing that determines our success. We can't allow one win to make us complacent. We need these wins to propel us further. Because our organizations are counting on each of us to ensure that the future of work is indeed inclusive.

As leaders, we need to understand that the future of work can only start to be inclusive if we commit to answering the following key question: How will you ensure the ways in which employees work with each other is inclusive? In this next section, we tackle this question head-on.

How Will You Ensure the Ways in Which Employees Work With Each Other Is Inclusive?

Hybrid work is no longer a futuristic term, a prediction of what work could look like. Hybrid work describes a flexible work model, which includes in-office employees, fully remote employees, and those employees who are some days in-office and some days work from home or offsite. It allows employees the freedom to choose where they want to work from to be the most productive. And hybrid work, a mix of onsite and remote work, is here to stay.

According to AT&T's Future of Work Study, their research shows that hybrid work will become the standard operating model updated by companies across industries. Here are three key insights to keep in mind from the AT&T study:

- 81 percent believe hybrid work will be the standard working model by 2024, with 56 percent of work done offsite.
- 72 percent of leaders surveyed lack a detailed hybrid model strategy and 76 percent don't have the right key performance indicators (KPIs) to support the model.
- 91 percent believe a hybrid work model will improve work-force diversity.[2]

Following are three things to keep in mind as you continue to adopt and embrace the hybrid work model when it comes to creating a more inclusive culture:

1. Build Everything You Do Putting Remote First.

Alicia Dietsch, Senior Vice President of AT&T Business Marketing, shared in the AT&T Future of Work Study the importance of putting remote first:

> "There's been a non-reversible shift in the way business is done thanks to the constraints of COVID-19. It's clear that a successful talent program now requires a hybrid work policy, but that policy needs to be supported by a strategic tech-first cultural reset, to ensure business growth and competition. Firms need to ask themselves if they have the in-house expertise to achieve this, or whether it's now time to go beyond a partner in remote infrastructure rollout to a partner in tech-first remote business strategy."[3]

As leaders, we must ensure that in everything we do, we have a tech-first remote strategy. When we do this, those who are remote are not an afterthought and don't feel excluded. When we build with remote in mind, we build an inclusive experience for all. This means considering all of the small and big moments at work:

- Ensuring that when you have a team offsite with a mix of in-person and remote attendees, that even those in the conference room join the video on their individual laptops.
- Making your annual company summit completely virtual so it is inclusive of all.
- Indicating in meeting invites "camera on" or "audio only."
- Offering recordings of key meetings, with closed captioning enabled.
- Sending lunch gift cards to those who are remote and can't enjoy the in-person lunch.
- Embracing asynchronous communication so no one has to be physically available or present as ideas, responses, or questions are being shared. Invest in asynchronous tools that help teams collaborate across different time zones and locations, including chat tools, file-sharing tools, and collaborative brainstorming tools.
- Aligning on key communication tools so employees don't feel bombarded by the same messaging on Slack, emails, texts, calls, FaceTime, WhatsApp, Microsoft Teams, or the next latest and greatest platform.

2. Ensure Someone Is Overseeing How Your Organization "Works."

There will continue to be a lot of experimentation, testing, and trying of new things when it comes to hybrid work. Understanding how your organization works and continuing to optimize and pivot ways of working in a hybrid model can become a full-time job. Some organizations are looking to hire someone who can oversee this work:

a Chief Remote Officer, Head of Remote Work, Chief Hybrid Work Officer.

Regardless of the title, the objective is the same: to ensure you don't rely on outdated strategies that worked at the beginning of the pandemic that no longer serve your employee base. If you can't afford the headcount currently, you should consider launching a standing committee where those tapped to serve have other projects taken off their plate. Also, this is not the job of your Chief Diversity Officer to take on alone, which we will discuss more in the next section.

Here are some key objectives when it comes to thinking about how your employees work:

- Identifying how your organization thinks about hybrid work and creating a playbook around how you expect individuals to work and show up. Creating a few metrics to start tracking over time will be key, including feedback from your employees on key initiatives and what's working and what's not.

    The following are some of the more specific hybrid work models to consider and how they may or may not foster inclusion:
    o Flexible hybrid model: employees choose when they want to work from home versus when they come in the office.
    o Fixed hybrid model: employees have set days when they can work remotely and set days when they come into the office.
    o Remote-first hybrid model: employees work remotely the majority of the time and travel to meet teams for in-person training or collaboration. Some organizations may be fully remote with no physical office space. Some may be remote first with limited office space and limited locations.
    o In-office first hybrid model: employees are expected to be in the office, with the option to work remotely from home a few days.

- Ensuring seamless onboarding and training for remote and hybrid workers so everyone has access to the same tools, in collaboration with recruiting and leadership and development.

- Collaborating with Human Resources to ensure everyone, including remote workers, are being paid fairly and equitably, including compensation, benefits, and perks (e.g., if you have office snacks and meals in the offices, send your remote workers a snack box or meal vouchers every quarter). You will want to consider if where the remote employee resides impacts their compensation, or if you are strictly looking at the role and skill set when it comes to compensation regardless of location.

- Leading with remote-first technology in collaboration with the Chief Technology Officer and ensuring cybersecurity education and training.

- Ensuring your in-person offices are set up with universal design in mind, to be inclusive of all people.

- Collaborating with recruiting to assess which roles can be remote and how to have access to more talent pools to increase diversity of representation.

- Continuously assessing how employees are communicating, focusing on the balance of optimizing asynchronous and synchronous work, studying work patterns of what work is done best independently versus whole collaborating, and observing the use of virtual formats versus in-person gatherings.

3. Finally, Ensure Hybrid Work Stays Inclusive for All

As we review Gallup's study on "The Advantages and Disadvantages of Hybrid Work," many of us can relate to the top advantages of hybrid work:

- Provides the flexibility for employees to work in ways that are effective for them.

- Improves their personal well-being and productivity at work.
- Can mitigate burnout and fatigue, offering better work/life balance.

The disadvantages of hybrid work noted in the study are:

- Lack of the right equipment, resources, and tools across teams in-office and offsite.
- Impaired collaboration and relationships, and disrupted work processes.
- Feeling less connected to the organization's culture.[4]

And I would argue, feeling less connected to the organization's culture may be exacerbated for those who identify as belonging to historically marginalized communities. Consider the following:

- According to The Future Forum's Remote Employee Experience Index, only 3 percent of Black knowledge employees want to return to full-time co-located work due to the everyday microaggressions they face in person.[5]
- As hate crimes against the Asian community continue to rise, many Asian colleagues may work remotely to put their safety first.[6]
- According to a Qualtrics study focusing on the challenges faced by parents working across industries, 42 percent of unemployed respondents said they would need full flexibility in choosing how and when they work if they were to consider to re-entering the workforce.[7]
- According to a *New York Times* study, the share of individuals with disabilities who are working soared in the past two years during the pandemic, given many organizations' newfound openness to remote work.[8]

- Finally, many LGBTQ+ professionals have admitted to feeling more secure with remote work, not feeling pressured to present themselves in a certain way.[9]

Ask yourself this: What does inclusivity mean for future of work if individuals predominantly from historically marginalized communities work remotely, and everyone else comes into the office? Are we actually being inclusive or are we unknowingly creating a two-tier system, where one group has more access, opportunity, and is more top-of-mind simply because they are in person?

And do we forget about everyone else simply because they are on a screen?

So when leading your hybrids teams, start by watching out for the following:

- <u>The rise of remote location or proximity bias.</u>

    This can be a preference for those who are in-office or come into the office more, with close physical proximity to leaders. They may be perceived as better workers and more committed. This bias can be reflected in performance ratings, compensation, and promotion opportunities when looking at in-office employees versus remote employees. Ensure you are monitoring and watching out for how this bias can play out.
- <u>The unintended impact of allowing employees to come into the office on the days they choose.</u>

    When we allow people to choose whatever days they want to come into the office, it reinforces flexibility and freedom. And yet, if employees come and go when they want, there may be less opportunity to build cross-cultural bridges, deepen relationships with existing team members, build relationships with new colleagues in person. Consider asking team members to come in on the same days or to get together in person for key moments of collaboration.

Consider this scenario: an employee who was hired remotely starts to come into the office. She sees that she's the only Black woman in the office, and no one is reaching out and connecting with her. Ensure the burden is not on this individual to meet people. Gone are the days when we might have the same desk at the office and be forced to get to know our neighbors. This is where office managers and the most senior leader in the office can play a role in facilitating introductions and scheduling lunches together to ensure no one feels excluded on the days they do come into the office, particularly for the first time.

■ The focus on diversity of representation for remote employees only.

With access to many more talent pools, organizations may be able to achieve diverse slates more quickly, as discussed in a prior chapter. But what happens when you have strong diversity of representation within your remote work population but within your in-office population, little to no diversity of representation? Be sure to look at the totality of your workforce when taking into consideration how your employees identify to monitor your progress on your diversity, equity, and inclusion efforts.

As leaders, don't forget that it's up to each of us to create a culture where everyone has an equal opportunity to thrive and can be successful in our hybrid world of work. We can't simply cling to the idea that "we can work from home now" and default to the idea that "the future of work is inclusive." We are responsible for ensuring we have the systems in place to build the groundwork for an inclusive future.

Conclusion: Now That We Have Debunked 13 Myths, Here's What Comes Next.

As the book comes to a close, let's address how we can stay committed to DEI efforts for the long-term. Once we have done the work of debunking these 13 myths, we need to ensure we don't lose momentum in our journey to be more inclusive leaders and build more inclusive organizations. Let's consider the following two questions:

1. How Will Your Organization Stay Committed to Your DEI Efforts Long Term?

While the work of diversity, equity, and inclusion work belongs to all of us, you also need a leader who can help oversee your efforts. If you are serious about this work, you need to have a Chief Diversity

Officer. If you are a smaller organization growing and scaling, you need someone spearheading this work. Again, if you are going to appoint people to a DEI council or committee, ensure other things are being taken off their plates and that being part of this council becomes part of their core job responsibilities.

Whether you are hiring someone for the first time, or are reimagining the current DEI structure, here are six questions you should ask yourself to ensure you are setting up the individual and your organization for success:

Why Now?

We have discussed that many organizations feel pressure from employees, customers, investors, and suppliers to get serious about DEI. But what, specifically, has changed for your company? Why are you now ready to hire a CDO when you weren't a year or three years ago, or elevate the current person overseeing your DEI efforts? Is there a new CEO, a new CHRO, and other new leaders in the C-Suite? Or did the existing executive team decide to make this a priority? Are you coming out of a crisis or trying to prevent one? Whatever the case, be upfront and honest about why you're ramping up your DEI efforts and where your organization is on its inclusion journey.

What Are the Job Requirements?

"The candidate should have 12 to 15 years of DEI experience, an advanced degree, and a track record of building and implementing an organizational inclusion roadmap." If your CDO job posting reads like that, it's time to stop and reassess. Take a moment to go back to the myth on recruiting talent. Ask yourself: What biases do you have about this role? What biases do you have about the skill set needed?

This is a newer area of focus for most of the business world: Corporate America started using diversity training only in the 1980s, to protect against civil rights lawsuits.[1] This is a growing field that hasn't always had the staffing, funding, and commitment it deserves. So instead of looking for direct senior DEI leadership experience, consider people with broader backgrounds but all the right skills: the ability to influence and be a change agent, to design strategy and deliver results, to create metrics and drive accountability, and to communicate effectively across all levels of the hierarchy. Those with marketing, sales, or communications backgrounds might be a great fit. Also consider people who have been informal D&I champions or, more specifically, have served as an executive sponsor for an Employee Resource Group. You don't have to be a career HR professional to do this work.

Where Does the Role Sit?

If your answer is three levels below the chief people officer, with little to no interaction with the CEO, then this role is not set up for success. The CDO should report directly to the CEO or to the head of HR with a dotted line to the CEO. Either way, a close partnership with HR, legal, and corporate communications with full access to and support from the entire C-Suite is critical. A CDO must have a seat at the senior leadership table if you want to see meaningful change. You can obtain buy-in by asking those executives to be part of the interview process and/or review of the current structure and ways of working.

What Size Budget and Team Will You Provide as Support?

A CDO does not wave a magic wand to transform an organization into an inclusive one overnight. Depending on the size of your company and your vision, the person will need dedicated resources: a budget is necessary to create a dedicated team. Do not expect your CDO to do all the strategic and operational work or personally train hundreds of employees on issues like unconscious bias. If you can't commit to this, you're probably not ready to have and support a chief diversity officer.

In small to mid-sized organizations, you might first bring in a CDO as an individual contributor to do a listening tour with employees and assess the current landscape. As this individual builds a strategy, they will need a budget commitment of at least $250,000-$500,000 to begin implementing best recruiting practices, improving trainings, and building external partnerships. Some of this budget may be shared with other stakeholders. Eventually, they will also need to make additional hires.

In large global organizations, with enterprise-wide initiatives, budgets will start in the $1 million plus range. CDOs will need a dedicated team of five people or more, depending on the size of the employee base, who bring varied knowledge and experiences, from partnering with diversity recruiters to create inclusive candidate experiences and pipelines to building supplier diversity programs. As discussed throughout this book, investing in strategic partnerships that help build bridges and access to diverse talent pools for early career, mid-career, as well as executives is critical.

Building an end-to-end inclusion ecosystem takes money, talent, and commitment.

What Metrics Will You Use to Track Success?

When we think about the role of a CDO, our biases start to kick in: They will host events and panels; support the development of Employee Resource Groups; intervene when racism, sexism, or homophobia rear their heads; and speak externally. But these can't be the only measures of success.

How will you track progress? Will you set workforce diversity targets with your legal team? Will you review key policies and practices, such as pay equity, paid parental leave, and bereavement leave, and commit to becoming an industry leader by signing on to external pledges? Will you tie executive compensation and recognition to those goals? Will you create a board of senior leaders to monitor DEI initiatives?

We know that what gets measured gets done. Be clear about what success in year one will look like. Take the time to go back through previous chapters mapping some of your key take-aways with where your organization currently is on its DEI journey. Maybe it is achieving a strong understanding of your workforce demographics and setting representation goals. Perhaps supplier diversity targets are set in year two. Pick a few key goals for organization and build on them every year.

Will the CDO Have Influence Over Your Products and Services?

Today, 40 percent of the U.S. population is non-white (Black/African American, Hispanic/Latinx, or Asian), and according to Nielsen, they have a spending power of $3.2 trillion.[2] One key focus area of the CDO should be to help build a workforce that represents the multicultural consumers your business serves. As we discussed earlier, equally important is understanding how your products and services show up in the marketplace.

Do you sell dark shades of foundations or bandages? Do you prominently feature Brown, Black, or racially ambiguous people in your marketing? Do you translate your content into Spanish or offer Hispanic-led programs? Do your products avoid cultural stereotyping? Do you work with diverse suppliers and vendors? The most effective CDOs are involved in not just HR but also innovation, operations, sales, and marketing to ensure their companies are authentically serving a diverse customer base inclusively and equitably.

If you think through these issues before hiring a CDO, or elevating your current role internally, the person you choose is less likely to become a figurehead or a check the box exercise. You will set the new hire and the organization up for success and drive the impact and change you want to see.

2. How Will You as a Leader Stay Committed to This Work?

More important than what the organization commits to is what we as leaders commit to do. Because we are the engines that run our organization. Don't forget that we are, in fact, the organization.

DEI fatigue sets in when this work is not shared and only owned by the chosen few. DEI fatigue sets in when there's economic instability, and DEI efforts are always the first to be cut. DEI fatigue sets in when we don't properly support our Chief Diversity Officers and their teams, and there's a revolving door of talent because they come to realize the organization isn't serious about this work. DEI fatigue sets in when we don't have KPIs and goals, when we don't track our progress in any shape or form. DEI fatigue sets in when there's a lack of accountability. And that lack of accountability starts with each and every one of us.

Finally, as we have covered throughout this book, DEI fatigue sets in when we hold on to myths that we believe help us make progress. When, in fact, these myths hold us back, and hinder us from transforming our workplaces. We get tired, overwhelmed, and exhausted. It can be easy to give up.

However, my challenge to you is this. Go back through each of the 13 myths we debunked. We spent time thinking about how as individuals we can be more inclusive leaders, the specific actions we can take in our workplaces and in our communities. On our journey to be more inclusive leaders, we have a responsibility to influence, impact, or, in some cases, help reconstruct the internal systems and processes to transform our workplaces, and what we do internally must match our external PR image.

Think about what resonated with you, what you learned about a myth the first time you read it, and what still makes you uncomfortable. Ask yourself the following:

- What are the three things I will personally commit to focusing on this year when it comes to being a more inclusive leader? Will you check back every quarter, do a self-audit on how you are progressing?
- How will I coach my colleagues and my teams to join me on this accountability journey? Will you ask each of them to also make three commitments?
- What are the three things I will ask my organization to commit to? How will you influence and help drive those organization-wide initiatives?
- How will I celebrate the small and big wins that will keep the momentum for this work going?
- Finally, how will I show up in those moments to bust workplace myths and educate my colleagues on what's really holding all of us back from building a more inclusive organization?

The future of work and of our organizations can only be inclusive if we commit to making this a priority. Holding on to these outdated workplace myths can only hurt our organizations and set back our well-intentioned efforts. We need to start reimagining what inclusion looks like in the small everyday moments, and in those bigger moments that play out across our organizations and show up in the marketplace. My sincere hope is that with the help of this book, you take on this challenge. As Margaret Mead once said, "Never doubt that a small group of thoughtful, committed citizens can change the world; indeed, it's the only thing that ever has."

If you are looking for that small group of thoughtful, committed leaders to transform your workplaces, look no further. Because you are that group. And we are waiting for you to get started.

Notes

Myth 1

1. https://www.diverseandengaged.com/tipping-point-live-event
2. https://shadowandact.com/lena-dunham-addresses-girls-diversity-criticism-why-i-just-dont-care
3. https://content.time.com/time/nation/article/0,8599,340694,00.html
4. https://www.mckinsey.com/featured-insights/gender-equality/focusing-on-what-works-for-workplace-diversity
5. https://www.eeoc.gov/statutes/title-vii-civil-rights-act-1964
6. https://www.wintersgroup.com/corporate-diversity-training-1964-to-present.pdf
7. https://www.google.com/books/edition/Workforce_2000/F9gwBesn1FoC?hl=en&gbpv=0
8. https://www.pnas.org/doi/10.1073/pnas.1908069116
9. https://www.elle.com/life-love/a33180/why-i-dont-love-blackgirlmagic/
10. https://spsp.org/news-center/character-context-blog/what-motivates-white-people-actively-support-black-lives-matter

11. https://www.washingtonpost.com/news/wonk/wp/2014/08/25/
three-quarters-of-whites-dont-have-any-non-white-friends/
12. https://www.reuters.com/article/us-usa-poll-race/many-
americans-have-no-friends-of-another-race-poll-idUSBRE977
04320130808?feedType=RSS&feedName=domesticNews
13. https://www.linkedin.com/in/mita-mallick-2b165822/
14. https://www.gartner.com/en/human-resources/glossary/employee-
resource-group-erg-

Myth 2

1. https://www.kornferry.com/insights/this-week-in-leadership/
the-inclusive-leader
2. https://www.catalyst.org/research/inclusive-leadership-report/
3. https://hbr.org/2020/03/the-key-to-inclusive-leadership
4. https://www2.deloitte.com/us/en/insights/topics/talent/six-
signature-traits-of-inclusive-leadership.html
5. Ibid.
6. https://www.cnbc.com/2017/10/11/how-to-combat-hepeating-
at-work-according-to-a-harvard-professor.html

Myth 3

1. https://www.merriam-webster.com/dictionary/courage
2. https://www.merriam-webster.com/dictionary/conversation
3. https://psychology.umbc.edu/wp-content/uploads/sites/57/
2016/10/White-Privilege_McIntosh-1989.pdf

Myth 4

1. https://www.cnn.com/2020/09/23/business/wells-fargo-ceo-
bias/index.html
2. https://apnews.com/article/race-and-ethnicity-census-2020-
vermont-721d8201122a857b4565b4a37bd77d24

3. https://www.protocol.com/bulletins/twitter-2021-diversity-report

4. https://www.bloomberg.com/news/articles/2022-01-12/twitter-leaned-on-work-from-anywhere-to-recruit-more-black-latinx-employees?leadSource=uverify%20wall#xj4y7vzkg

5. https://www.benefitnews.com/news/new-pwc-workplace-equity-commitment-to-support-black-latinx-students

6. https://www.oprahdaily.com/life/a33395013/latino-vs-hispanic-meaning/

7. https://www.merriam-webster.com/words-at-play/word-history-latinx

8. https://www.pewresearch.org/hispanic/2020/08/11/about-one-in-four-u-s-hispanics-have-heard-of-latinx-but-just-3-use-it/

9. https://ncses.nsf.gov/pubs/nsf19304/digest/introduction

10. https://www.nytimes.com/2020/06/26/us/black-african-american-style-debate.html

11. https://www.usatoday.com/story/news/nation/2019/06/29/latina-latino-latinx-hispanic-what-do-they-mean/1596501001/

12. https://www.healthline.com/health/native-american-vs-american-indian#term-origins

13. https://operations.nfl.com/inside-football-ops/inclusion/the-rooney-rule/

14. https://hbr.org/2016/04/if-theres-only-one-woman-in-your-candidate-pool-theres-statistically-no-chance-shell-be-hired

15. https://time.com/6145755/brian-flores-lawsuit-rooney-rule-diversity/

16. https://www.nytimes.com/2022/05/19/business/wells-fargo-fake-interviews.html

17. https://www.starbucks.com/careers/working-at-starbucks/culture-and-values/

18. https://about.google/philosophy/
19. https://www.wholefoodsmarket.com/mission-values/core-values

Myth 5

1. https://www.eeoc.gov/harassment
2. https://www.netflix.com/tudum/articles/the-story-behind-abercrombie-and-fitchs-anti-asian-t-shirts
3. https://www.stopbullying.gov/bullying/what-is-bullying
4. https://workplacebullying.org/2021-wbi-survey/
5. https://hrdailyadvisor.blr.com/2019/07/17/pitfalls-of-zero-tolerance-policies/
6. https://www.nytimes.com/2020/05/26/nyregion/amy-cooper-dog-central-park.html
7. https://workplacebullying.org/2021-wbi-survey/
8. https://hbr.org/2020/05/if-something-feels-off-you-need-to-speak-up

Myth 6

1. https://www.pewresearch.org/fact-tank/2023/03/01/gender-pay-gap-facts/
2. https://www.census.gov/library/stories/2022/03/what-is-the-gender-wage-gap-in-your-state.html
3. https://www.americanprogress.org/article/women-of-color-and-the-wage-gap/
4. https://www.nami.org/Your-Journey/Identity-and-Cultural-Dimensions/Asian-American-and-Pacific-Islander
5. https://www.americanprogress.org/article/economic-status-asian-american-pacific-islander-women/
6. https://www.cnbc.com/2021/05/20/aapi-women-have-the-smallest-pay-gapbut-that-doesnt-tell-the-full-story.html

7. https://www.americanprogress.org/article/women-of-color-and-the-wage-gap/

8. https://fortune.com/2018/04/09/equal-pay-companies-starbucks-apple/

9. https://www.businesswire.com/news/home/20190826005390/en/More-Than-Half-of-Americans-Avoid-Discussing-Personal-Finances-eMoney-Advisor-Study-Finds

10. https://www.businessinsider.com/data-americans-dont-talk-about-money-with-friends-2021-6

11. https://hbr.org/2020/11/how-to-identify-and-fix-pay-inequality-at-your-company

12. https://www.ciphr.com/features/unconscious-bias-in-the-workplace/

13. https://carta.com/equity-summit/reports/2021/?ces=1

14. https://www.businessinsider.com/reddit-policy-on-not-negotiating-salaries-2015-5

15. https://www.shrm.org/resourcesandtools/hr-topics/compensation/pages/marketpricing.aspx

16. https://hbr.org/2020/07/whats-your-negotiation-strategy

17. https://nwlc.org/wp-content/uploads/2020/05/Moms-EPD-2020-v2.pdf

18. https://www.usatoday.com/story/life/allthemoms/2019/06/10/wage-gap-widens-between-working-moms-and-dads-nwlc-moms-equal-pay-day/1344822001/

19. https://www.pewresearch.org/fact-tank/2019/05/08/facts-about-u-s-mothers/

20. https://nwlc.org/wp-content/uploads/2020/05/Moms-EPD-2020-v2.pdf

21. https://www.sciencedaily.com/releases/2018/06/180614213621.htm

22. https://www.thirdway.org/report/the-fatherhood-bonus-and-the-motherhood-penalty-parenthood-and-the-gender-gap-in-pay

23. https://www.tuc.org.uk/sites/default/files/Pay_and_Parenthood_ Touchstone_Extra_2016_LR.pdf

24. https://www.cnbc.com/2019/04/30/first-time-moms-see-a- 30percent-drop-in-pay-for-dads-theres-a-bump-up.html

25. https://www.cnbc.com/2020/01/31/women-more-likely-to- change-jobs-to-get-pay-increase.html

26. https://www.census.gov/newsroom/stories/equal-pay-day.html

27. https://www.aauw.org/resources/article/equal-pay-day-calendar/

Myth 7

1. https://www.forbes.com/sites/forbescommunicationscouncil/ 2022/05/19/does-mentoring-still-matter-for-fortune-500- companies/?sh=e92ea265d8c7

2. https://hbr.org/2020/07/why-your-mentorship-program- isnt-working

3. https://www.nationalgeographic.com/culture/article/asian- american-model-minority-myth-masks-history-discrimination

4. https://www.nami.org/Your-Journey/Identity-and-Cultural- Dimensions/Asian-American-and-Pacific-Islander

5. https://clp.law.harvard.edu/knowledge-hub/magazine/

6. https://www.census.gov/library/stories/2021/08/improved- race-ethnicity-measures-reveal-united-states-population-much- more-multiracial.html

7. https://www.shrm.org/hr-today/news/all-things-work/pages/ racism-corporate-america.aspx

8. https://www.census.gov/library/stories/2021/08/improved- race-ethnicity-measures-reveal-united-states-population-much- more-multiracial.html

9. https://www.brookings.edu/blog/the-avenue/2018/03/14/ the-us-will-become-minority-white-in-2045-census-projects/

10. https://www.census.gov/library/stories/2021/08/improved-race-ethnicity-measures-reveal-united-states-population-much-more-multiracial.html

11. https://www.latimes.com/opinion/story/2021-05-06/asian-bias-discrimination-corporate-culture-glass-ceiling

12. https://hbr.org/2018/05/asian-americans-are-the-least-likely-group-in-the-u-s-to-be-promoted-to-management

13. https://www.pewresearch.org/social-trends/2018/01/09/women-and-men-in-stem-often-at-odds-over-workplace-equity/

14. https://store.hbr.org/product/the-sponsor-effect-how-to-be-a-better-leader-by-investing-in-others/10194

Myth 8

1. https://hbr.org/2020/11/maternity-leave-isnt-enough-to-retain-new-moms

2. https://www.shrm.org/hr-today/trends-and-forecasting/research-and-surveys/pages/national-study-of-employers.aspx

3. https://www.shrm.org/resourcesandtools/hr-topics/benefits/pages/how-much-parental-leave-is-too-much.aspx

4. https://hbr.org/2017/07/a-winning-parental-leave-policy-can-be-surprisingly-simple

5. https://www.glassdoor.com/blog/companies-redefining-parental-leave/

6. https://hbr.org/2020/03/two-new-moms-return-to-work-one-in-seattle-one-in-stockholm

7. https://www.thesecondshift.com/about-us/

8. https://hbr.org/2018/09/do-longer-maternity-leaves-hurt-womens-careers

9. https://www.marketwatch.com/story/tech-companies-are-offering-parents-additional-benefits-as-covid-19-threatens-schools-return-11596505660

10. https://www.pewresearch.org/fact-tank/2022/05/06/working-moms-in-the-u-s-have-faced-challenges-on-multiple-fronts-during-the-pandemic/

11. https://qz.com/work/806516/the-secret-to-patagonias-success-keeping-moms-and-onsite-child-care-and-paid-parental-leave

12. https://modernhire.com/bias-in-hiring-part-two-of-four/

13. https://www.mckinsey.com/featured-insights/diversity-and-inclusion/women-in-the-workplace

14. https://www.unilever.com/planet-and-society/equity-diversity-and-inclusion/gender-equality-and-womens-empowerment/

15. https://www.dol.gov/sites/dolgov/files/WB/media/Two%20Years%20into%20the%20Pandemic_Women%20Ages%2065.pdf

16. https://www.theglobeandmail.com/canada/article-lisa-laflamme-ctv-grey-hair/

17. https://www.aarp.org/health/conditions-treatments/info-2022/women-discrimination-and-mental-health.html

18. https://www.forbes.com/sites/ellevate/2020/11/02/working-womens-double-dose-of-discrimination-gender--ageism/?sh=3a8bbc661d19

Myth 9

1. https://www.nytimes.com/interactive/2020/09/09/us/powerful-people-race-us.html

2. https://finance.yahoo.com/news/white-men-account-72-corporate-212102494.html?guce_referrer=aHR0cHM6Ly93d3cuZ29vZ2xlLmNvbS8&guce_referrer_sig=AQAAAFwf7fzIzs6DDsgbHaKZl4T1auJZ8pxvxuo_s-nXMJtZCBrJiIb_k0zp-Rp5dNzZ3fV8ahorKKoTURMgmdLh2c8WFAuvs3smelvzqQ2jR9aGxSTUGKBFFTzI0wrB1OYZf7mv6lPG9ylPmn7Z3N5U07N7sjv_SJ10ejAr_tSNeK3y&guccounter=2

3. https://www.cnbc.com/2020/10/13/pandemic-fallout-men-got-3-times-more-promotions-than-women.html

4. https://www.prnewswire.com/news-releases/what-do-white-men-really-think-about-diversity-and-inclusion-in-the-workplace-301104952.html

5. https://www.greatheartconsulting.com/chuckshelton

6. https://www.mckinsey.com/featured-insights/diversity-and-inclusion/one-move-companies-can-take-to-improve-diversity

7. https://www.mckinsey.com/featured-insights/diversity-and-inclusion/diversity-wins-how-inclusion-matters

8. https://www.mckinsey.com/featured-insights/diversity-and-inclusion

9. https://www.nielsen.com/insights/2018/the-database-meeting-todays-multicultural-consumers/

10. https://www.glassdoor.com/employers/blog/diversity/

11. https://www.tinypulse.com/blog/17-surprising-statistics-about-employee-retention

12. https://www.cnbc.com/2022/04/01/less-than-25percent-of-black-employees-feel-included-at-work-what-companies-can-be-doing-better.html

13. https://www.tinypulse.com/blog/17-surprising-statistics-about-employee-retention

14. https://ssir.org/articles/entry/the_curb_cut_effect

15. Ibid.

16. https://www.mckinsey.com/capabilities/people-and-organizational-performance/our-insights/a-fresh-look-at-paternity-leave-why-the-benefits-extend-beyond-the-personal

17. https://coara.co/blog/corporate-accelerator-programs

Myth 10

1. https://www.urbandictionary.com/define.php?term=Rainbow-washing

2. https://parade.com/1048962/lindsaylowe/rainbow-pride-flag-meaning-history/

3. http://www.lgbt-capital.com/docs/Estimated_LGBT-GDP_%28table%29_-_July_2015.pdf

4. https://www.cbsnews.com/news/gay-pride-2019-rainbow-retail-a-big-business-opportunity-in-pride-month-and-beyond/

5. https://reports.hrc.org/corporate-equality-index-2022

6. https://campaigns.organizefor.org/petitions/help-make-hair-discrimination-illegal

7. https://www.bbc.com/news/world-us-canada-54566087

8. https://nypost.com/2021/04/14/disney-adopts-gender-inclusive-costumes-for-theme-park-staff/

9. https://www.cnn.com/travel/article/black-santa-disney-parks/index.html

10. https://www.wdwinfo.com/disney-merchandise/disneys-rainbow-collection-what-why-how-this-is-more-than-just-another-line-of-merchandise/

11. https://www.npr.org/2022/03/22/1088048998/disney-walkout-dont-say-gay-bill

12. https://thewaltdisneycompany.com/statement-on-disneys-support-for-the-lgbtq-community/

13. https://www.opensecrets.org/political-action-committees-pacs/what-is-a-pac

14. https://docs.google.com/forms/d/e/1FAIpQLSdKVfRFgdV7XQJiiVuZFTIiuTJU62LBb80kMGSlXHdGyv5VXA/viewform

15. https://www.glaad.org/sri/2019/walt-disney-studios

16. https://www.latimes.com/entertainment-arts/movies/story/2020-03-10/onward-lgbtq-representation-disney-pixar

17. https://variety.com/2022/film/news/disney-pixar-same-sex-affection-censorship-dont-say-gay-bill-1235200582/

18. https://www.wdwinfo.com/disney-merchandise/disneys-rainbow-collection-what-why-how-this-is-more-than-just-another-line-of-merchandise/

19. https://thewaltdisneycompany.com/disney-earns-top-score-in-hrc-foundation-corporate-equality-index/
20. https://www.hrc.org/press-releases/human-rights-campaign-refuses-money-from-disney-until-meaningful-action-is-taken-to-combat-floridas-dont-say-gay-or-trans-bill
21. https://martechseries.com/content/getty-images-and-glaad-challenge-global-creatives-to-break-visual-stereotypes-faced-by-the-lgbtq-community/
22. https://hypebeast.com/2019/5/harrys-pride-month-special-shaving-kit
23. https://www.coca-colacompany.com/news/coca-cola-fosters-inclusive-lgbtq-community
24. https://www.ibm.com/impact/be-equal/communities/lgbtq/
25. https://www.protocol.com/bulletins/linkedin-will-pay-10-000-to-erg-leaders

Myth 11

1. https://www.mprnews.org/story/2016/04/13/sprint-pulls-ghetto-ad
2. https://nypost.com/2016/04/13/sprints-pulls-ghetto-commercial-amid-backlash/
3. Ibid.
4. https://time.com/4997485/kelloggs-corn-pops-cereal-boxes-racism-saladin-ahmed/
5. https://www.theguardian.com/world/2017/oct/08/dove-apologises-for-ad-showing-black-woman-turning-into-white-one
6. https://www.chicagotribune.com/dining/ct-we-tried-hellmanns-pride-rainbow-sprinkle-mayo-grilled-cheese-story.html

7. https://www.thelily.com/diors-sauvage-ad-which-paired-a-racial-stereotype-with-an-image-of-a-native-american-has-been-pulled-from-social-media/

8. https://www.cbsnews.com/news/h-m-the-weeknd-coolest-monkey-in-the-jungle-racist-hoodie/

9. https://www.fastcompany.com/90602465/the-internet-noticed-whats-wrong-with-the-nfls-anti-racism-super-bowl-ad

10. https://www.npr.org/2022/10/05/1126883325/the-great-british-bake-off-mexico-week-backlash

11. https://www.edelman.com/sites/g/files/aatuss191/files/2022-06/2022%20Edelman%20Trust%20Barometer%20Special%20Report%20The%20New%20Cascade%20of%20Influence%20FINAL.pdf

12. https://www.cnbc.com/video/2022/02/01/black-spending-power-reaches-record-1-point-6-trillion-but-net-worth-falls.html

13. https://us.pg.com/blogs/multicultural-growth/

14. https://www.voguebusiness.com/fashion/dolce-and-gabbana-and-donatella-versace-talk-plus-size-fashion

15. https://www.today.com/style/forget-plus-size-models-have-chosen-new-word-describe-their-t60441

16. https://www.thecrownact.com/

17. https://www.adweek.com/brand-marketing/the-adidas-x-soul-cap-partnership-why-it-works/

18. https://www.benjerry.com/about-us/media-center/dismantle-white-supremacy

19. https://www.opentoall.com/sephora-racial-bias-study/

20. https://www.adweek.com/brand-marketing/its-time-brands-include-black-santa/

21. https://www.cnn.com/videos/business/2020/08/14/good-humor-rza-ice-cream-orig.cnn-business

22. https://www.pgcareers.com/mbib-thetalk-video
23. https://nmaahc.si.edu/explore/stories/blackface-birth-american-stereotype
24. https://www.blackhistorycultureacademy.com/home
25. https://www.ferris.edu/news/jimcrow/tom/
26. https://oyc.yale.edu/african-american-studies/afam-162
27. https://ldhi.library.cofc.edu/exhibits/show/hidden-voices/enslaved-women-and-slaveholder/sexual-violence
28. https://www.wired.com/story/a-genealogy-sites-racist-ad-tumbles-into-a-cultural-minefield/
29. https://www.brown.edu/news/2016-01-07/shackles
30. https://www.npr.org/sections/thetwo-way/2012/06/19/155348916/adidas-cancels-its-shackle-shoes
31. https://nmaahc.si.edu/explore/stories/blackface-birth-american-stereotype
32. https://www.cnn.com/2019/02/07/us/gucci-blackface-sweater
33. https://www.nytimes.com/2019/02/12/style/katy-perry-blackface-shoes.html
34. https://www.essence.com/fashion/clothing/moncler-racist-blackface-jacket/
35. https://www.learningforjustice.org/magazine/the-disturbing-monkey-business-of-us-blackwhite-race-relations
36. https://time.com/5480583/prada-blackface/
37. https://www.nbcnews.com/news/nbcblk/reckoning-dr-seuss-racist-imagery-has-been-years-making-n1259330
38. https://nypost.com/2021/03/02/six-dr-seuss-books-wont-be-published-for-racist-images/
39. https://www.ferris.edu/jimcrow/mammies/
40. https://www.today.com/tmrw/how-minstrel-shows-1800s-led-us-racist-stereotypes-culture-today-t185341

41. https://www.cleveland.com/entertainment/2020/06/mrs-butterworths-syrup-is-consdering-changing-its-branding-and-packaging-too.html
42. https://www.npr.org/2021/02/10/966166648/aunt-jemima-no-more-pancake-brand-renamed-pearl-milling-company
43. https://thedieline.com/blog/2022/9/6/conagra-brands-said-they-would-change-the-mrs-butterworths-bottle-so-what-happened?
44. https://www.ferris.edu/news/jimcrow/tom/
45. https://files.nc.gov/dncr-moh/jim%20crow%20etiquette.pdf
46. https://www.wsj.com/articles/uncle-bens-changes-brand-rooted-in-racist-imagery-now-its-bens-original-11600848000
47. https://www.today.com/food/uncle-ben-s-now-ben-s-original-rebranded-rice-hits-t218156
48. https://www.rollingstone.com/culture/culture-news/cream-of-wheat-branding-racism-1017004/
49. https://www.usatoday.com/story/money/food/2020/09/26/cream-of-wheat-box-black-chef-removal-2021/3546813001/
50. https://www.ncbi.nlm.nih.gov/pmc/articles/PMC4365794/
51. https://www.newsweek.com/nivea-ad-causes-backlash-687965
52. https://www.businessinsider.com/heineken-pulls-racist-lighter-is-better-campaign-2018-3
53. https://www.today.com/food/ugly-ducking-chocolate-causes-racist-controversy-grocery-store-t151877
54. https://www.history.com/news/why-is-the-south-known-as-dixie
55. https://www.goodhousekeeping.com/life/entertainment/a32972406/dixie-chicks-name-change-the-chicks/
56. https://www.historynet.com/antebellum-period/?r
57. https://www.axios.com/2020/06/11/lady-antebellum-name-change-slavery

58. https://www.billboard.com/business/legal/lady-antebellum-a-name-change-lawsuits-settlement-1235025794/

59. https://narrative.colorofchange.org/?utm_source=colorofchange_org

60. https://www.washingtoninformer.com/cdc-study-shatters-myth-about-black-fathers/

61. https://www.yahoo.com/video/burt-bees-apologizes-family-christmas-234500123.html

62. https://www.cnn.com/2018/06/14/us/target-greeting-card

63. https://narrative.colorofchange.org/?utm_source=colorofchange_org

Myth 12

1. https://www.edelman.com/sites/g/files/aatuss191/files/2022-01/2022%20Edelman%20Trust%20Barometer%20Global%20Report_Final.pdf

2. https://www.insider.com/tiktok-disability-community-forgave-lizzo-ableist-slur-2022-6

3. https://stories.starbucks.com/press/2018/starbucks-ceo-reprehensible-outcome-in-philadelphia-incident /

4. https://www.cfo.com/corporate-finance/2020/12/starbucks-to-tie-executive-pay-to-diversity-goals/#:~:text=Starbucks%20said%20it%20will%20tie,the%20corporate%20level%20by%202025

5. https://stories.starbucks.com/uploads/2020/10/Starbucks-Workforce-Demographics-Data-Description-August-2020.pdf

6. https://www.usatoday.com/story/money/2018/01/08/h-m-apologizes-ad-showing-black-child-model-wearing-monkey-hoodie/1012309001/

7. https://www.refinery29.com/en-us/2019/07/237347/h-m-racist-hoodie-controversy-diversity-problem

8. https://www.vox.com/the-goods/2019/6/13/18677563/sephora-sza-ulta-racial-bias-shopping-while-black

9. https://fortune.com/longform/sephora-racial-bias-in-retail-report/

10. https://newsroom.sephora.com/28-major-u-s-retailer-brands-form-charter-to-improve-retail-environment-by-mitigating-racially-biased-experiences/

11. https://www.nytimes.com/2020/06/10/business/sephora-black-owned-brands.html

12. https://15percentpledge.org/

13. https://www.lawnmowerlawnmower.com/se-news/pdf/External%20-%20Final%20Sephora%20DEI%20Heart%20Journey%20Report%202022-compressed.pdf

14. https://www.cnn.com/2022/07/19/us/sesame-place-apology-rosita-black-girls-backlash-reaj/index.html

15. https://www.npr.org/2022/07/19/1112234153/sesame-place-apology-backlash-racism-rosita

16. https://www.cnn.com/2022/07/19/us/sesame-place-apology-rosita-black-girls-backlash-reaj/index.html

17. https://sesameplace.com/philadelphia/-/media/sesame-place-langhorne/files/pdf/2022_spl_announces-actions-to-advance-dei-pr.ashx?la=en&hash=6AAAB1BE2C0A3E13DEE0C80D83CB939F729F5117&version=1_202208093134&hash=6AAAB1BE2C0A3E13DEE0C80D83CB939F729F5117

Myth 13

1. https://www.mckinsey.com/capabilities/people-and-organizational-performance/our-insights/reimagining-the-office-and-work-life-after-covid-19

2. https://about.att.com/story/2022/future-of-work-study-results.html

3. Ibid.
4. https://www.gallup.com/workplace/398135/advantages-challenges-hybrid-work.aspx
5. https://futureforum.com/2021/03/11/dismantling-the-office-moving-from-retrofit-to-redesign/
6. https://hbr.org/2022/03/do-your-aapi-employees-feel-safe-coming-back-to-work
7. https://www.qualtrics.com/blog/new-world-of-work-flexibility/?utm_medium=social&utm_source=twitter&utm_campaign=pr-study&utm_content=boardlist-2021
8. https://www.nytimes.com/2022/10/25/business/economy/labor-disabilities.html
9. https://www.turing.com/blog/remote-work-for-lgbtq-in-tech-pride-month-2022/

Conclusion

1. https://diversityofficermagazine.com/cultural-diversity-factoids/historical-issues/
2. https://www.nielsen.com/insights/2018/the-database-meeting-todays-multicultural-consumers/

Acknowledgments

Those who believe anything I write is amazing:

My mother, Manjula, has read almost everything I have written. And in those moments when I stopped writing, she encouraged me to keep writing. While she says she is proud to be my mother, I am even prouder to be her daughter.

My brother, Sumit, has always been one of my biggest allies and confidantes. Next to my mother, he has read almost everything I have ever written. My sister-in-law, Allison, for her and my brother's feedback and coaching on the book and engaging our kids in activities while I made final edits!

My husband, Piyush, has supported my dream of becoming a writer since the day we met. He never lets me forget my worth, even in the moments I start to doubt my capabilities. I look forward to the day our kids, Jay and Priya, read this book.

Finally, while my dad is no longer here with us, I imagine him sitting in his red chair, sipping a cup of tea while proudly reading this book. He always encouraged me to follow my passion for writing. It's because of my parents' unwavering support that this book became a reality.

I love you all.

Those who believed I could write this book:

Dee C. Marshall, Sarah Solomon-Mason, Josh Getzler, Julie Kerr, Victoria Savanh, Alexandra Carter

Those who believed my childhood dream of writing a book would come true:

Asha Santos, Diana Santiago, Danni Maggin, Charli Long Spellane, Tara Deshpande, Catherine Borda de Castro, Nisha Thomas Dearborn

Those who helped me find and believe in my voice again:

Christy DeSantis, Lan Phan, Jill Katz, Madhura Phadke, Katie Burke, LaQuanda Murray, Carol Watson, Gail Tifford, Jonathan Atwood, Gina Boswell, Claude Silver, Smita Reddy, Lisa Sepulveda, Cate Luzio, Tracy Avin, Monica Marcel, Chuck Adams, Subha Barry, Callie Schweitzer, Jennifer Teitler, Jacqueline Warren, Wendy Leshgold, Lisa Shalett, Josh Saterman, Sonali Pai, Lisa Hurley, Elizabeth Leiba, Daisy Lovelace, Jessi Hempel, Mike Nussbaum, Rich Cardona, Warren Zarate

And to all those who have supported me on my journey. You know who you are. I am grateful for your friendship, love, and support.

Now that I found my voice again, I'll never stop using it.

About the Author

Mita Mallick is a corporate change-maker with a track record of transforming businesses. She gives innovative ideas a voice and serves customers and communities with purpose. She has had an extensive career as a marketer in the beauty and consumer product goods space, being a fierce advocate of including and representing Black and Brown communities.

Her passion for inclusive storytelling led her to become a Chief Diversity Officer, to build end-to-end inclusion ecosystems across big and small organizations. Mallick has brought her talent and expertise to companies like Carta, Unilever, Pfizer, AVON, Johnson & Johnson, and more. She's a sought-after speaker and coach to startup founders, executives, and public CEOs.

Mallick is a LinkedIn Top Voice, a contributor for *Harvard Business Review*, *Adweek*, *Entrepreneur*, and *Fast Company*. Mallick has been featured in *The New York Times*, *The Washington Post*, *Time*, *Forbes*, *Axios*, *Essence*, *Cosmopolitan*, and *Business Insider*. She was featured in a documentary created by Soledad O'Brien Productions for CBS News entitled *Women in the Workplace: The Unfinished Fight for Equality*. Mallick holds a BA from Barnard College, Columbia University, and an MBA from Duke University's Fuqua School of Business. She lives in New Jersey with her husband and two children.

Index